The Fearless Mindset

The Entrepreneur's Guide to Get Fit in Less Time, Double Your Income, and Become Unstoppable

Peter L. Scott, IV

Contents

The Fearless Mindset: The Entrepreneur's Guide to Get Fit in Less Time, Double Your Income, and Become Unstoppable.

Disclaimer & FTC Notice

While all attempts have been made to verify the information provided in this publication, neither the author nor the publisher assumes any responsibility for errors, omissions, or contrary interpretations of the subject matter herein.

This book is for informational purposes only. The

Dedication

This book is dedicated to my mother and father who taught me to live fearlessly and love with all my being.

To my grandparents, who taught me to be self-reliant.

To my sister, who taught me the power of perseverance.

And to Sean Stephenson for helping me find the message inside my painful past.

IMPORTANT:
Before You Continue...

<u>Your Free Gift</u>

As a way of saying thank you for purchasing this book, I'm offering you the following free book bonuses:

- The Unstoppable Entrepreneur quiz
- The Fearless Fitness Challenge four-part video series
- Expert interviews with the world's fittest entrepreneurs
- The Fearless Life goal/habit tracking sheet

For exclusive access to these bonuses, go to www.thefearlessmindsetbook.com

Introduction:

Achieving the Life You Deserve and Desire

There are millions of entrepreneurs like you and me who have a burning desire to skyrocket the growth of their businesses to create a greater impact in the world and make more money because of it. Yet most entrepreneurs fail to reach their potential and achieve their financial and personal goals because of two key constraints: fear and misaligned priorities. First, they allow their fears, doubts, and limiting beliefs to slow them down or stop them from taking the action required to achieve their goals. Second, they spend every waking moment working on their business, thereby neglecting their health, relationships, and every other area of their life.

The reality is that waiting for your fears to disappear keeps you from creating the life you deserve and desire right now. Waiting to be more courageous before taking action is limiting you from creating the life you deserve. And misaligning your priorities massively undermines the energy, focus, and confidence you need to create the most value in your business and skyrocket your income.

The world is changing faster than ever before. On one hand, today is the best time in history to become an entrepreneur with the greatest opportunity. On the other hand, the rapid growth of technology is radically transforming the entrepreneurial landscape by removing barriers to entry, which has led to unprecedented levels of competition.

In order for today's entrepreneur to achieve their life goals, they have to be more than just successful in business. The house in the suburbs and two cars that used to be the American Dream has now become the American Nightmare. Success is no longer defined simply by wealth. Although wealth is a key component of success and happiness, it's not the only thing.

If you're like most entrepreneurs, you've made significant sacrifices to get to where you are right now. You've missed your kids Little League games. You've canceled on date night with your spouse. You've hit snooze and skipped your morning workout because you were burning the midnight oil in your business.

This doesn't only apply to entrepreneurs. This sacrifice is common for anyone who is committed to being successful in their career. And although some level of sacrifice is undoubtedly required as you pursue your dreams, being maniacally obsessed with your career severely impairs your quality of life. Obsession is a good thing when harnessed and focused in the right capacity. But blind obsession? That can be devastating to one's life.

To be sure, something is missing in the life of the modern-day entrepreneur—a sense of happiness and fulfillment. The concept of balance has become more of a far-fetched dream than a reality. It is something that the "self-help gurus" preach from stage, but rarely live themselves. So the modern entrepreneur is left to wonder, "Is it really possible? Is it possible to reach my financial goals while becoming healthy, vibrant, happy, joyful, and fulfilled in all other areas of my life?" My answer is a resounding yes!

But in order to achieve your fullest potential in all areas of life, you must first develop a fearless mindset.

Now what is a fearless mindset you ask? A fearless mindset is a way of viewing yourself and the world around you. It includes a set of foundational, non-negotiable beliefs and attitudes that propel you to take on new challenges and keep moving forward despite obstacles so you can become an unstoppable entrepreneur. Chapter 5, "Becoming Unstoppable," will list ten such beliefs and explain in detail exactly how to go about acquiring those beliefs yourself.

I learned by interviewing some of the world's most successful entrepreneurs that the secret to creating a fearless mindset is all about how you live your daily life. It's the choices and actions you make every single day that make up your life. It's what you do and think that propels you toward or repels you from your life vision. Building the right daily habits and rituals will help skyrocket your energy, focus, and confidence and allow you to handle any adversity you encounter. The fearless mindset will empower you to live courageously despite your fears, doubts, and limiting beliefs.

When you have a fearless mindset, you'll not only succeed in business, but you'll be able to achieve balance in your life. This book will teach you how to create a fearless mindset so that as a busy entrepreneur you can get fit in less time, double your income, and become unstoppable.

Who Is This Book For?

This book is primarily for overworked and overwhelmed entrepreneurs. It is designed for entrepreneurs who are exhausted and frustrated by the demanding lifestyle they have built for themselves. This book is for entrepreneurs who are neglecting all other areas of their lives (their health, love relationship, parenting) in pursuit of their financial goals.

Although this book is written as an entrepreneurs guide, the principles and strategies can be applied to anyone who wants to create an extraordinary life for themselves and their family. It is relevant to stay-at-home parents who are consumed by raising and caring for their children. It is relevant to employees who are struggling to find balance with their demanding work schedule.

Above all, this book is for people who are highly committed to overcoming their fears, doubts, and limiting beliefs. They know that they could be living a life at a higher level, but they have allowed their fears to consume them and limit them from taking action.

As important as it is for me to define whom this book is for, it's even more important to define whom this book is not for!

This book is not for the weak-willed, lazy, or faint of heart. It is not for people who are comfortable settling for a mundane existence, nor is it for victims who blame their parents, their partner, the fact they grew up poor, or their genetics for their present circumstances.

This doesn't mean you can't be struggling— anyone who has achieved greatness has had to overcome immense challenges in life. Rather, what this means is that you take responsibility for your current reality and are committed to taking action to create the life you want to live today, regardless of your current circumstances!

Simply put, this book is for you if you're committed to becoming the badass you were born to be!

Who Is This Peter Scott IV Guy?

You might be saying to yourself, "Okay, this sounds

great and all, Peter, but who are you and why should I listen to you?"

Well, first off, even though I'm the fourth generation Peter Scott, I don't necessarily run my own dynasty. However, I am highly committed to upholding the integrity of my father's, grandfather's, and great-grandfather's name.

In fact, that's been a priority for me since my twelfth birthday, when I received a framed newspaper clipping of the following poem:

You got it from your father
It was all he had to give
So it's yours to use and cherish
For as long as you may live.
If you lose the watch he gave you
It can always be replaced.
But a black mark on your name, son,
Can never be erased.
It was clean the day you took it
And a worthy name to bear
When he got it from his father,
There was no dishonor there.

So make sure you guard it wisely,
After all is said and done
You'll be glad the name is spotless
When you give it to your son.
—Anonymous

From the moment I first read those words, I became committed to living a life of integrity.

Now, although my family loves me unconditionally, there are moments when they are terrified of my public vulnerability and they discourage me from my mission out of fear of leaving a black mark on our family name.

But my commitments are bigger than my family's fears. So I continue today to speak authentically and vulnerably to share my message with the world. And I challenge you to stop sacrificing your dreams to make other people comfortable.

Roman numerals aside, I'm Peter Scott and I've been mentoring and coaching high-achieving entrepreneurs since 2010.

As an ex-investment banker turned entrepreneur, I've

experienced the downside of neglecting every area of my personal life in pursuit of financial freedom. My health and relationships fell apart as I logged ninety-hour workweeks. I experienced rapid weight gain, limited energy, and mental fog. And I learned that it's impossible to build a successful business when the rest of your life is a total mess.

Below is a parable I wrote about my transformational journey from miserable investment banker to fearless entrepreneur:

What do you believe is the fundamental difference between these two men?

One is an investment banker (on the left) who is chained to a cubicle crunching numbers in Excel for ninety hours per week. He makes more money than most people his age, but he is miserable.

He is living a lie …

On the outside, he portrays what his family and society taught him to believe is success. But on the inside, he is empty.

He is disconnected from his purpose and is sleep walking through his life. He doesn't take time to care for his body and the effects are beginning to show.

If he continues on this path, what will he be remembered for? Sure, his family will approve of his safe and secure job, but is that the only meaning of life?

Now he may be smiling … but do you think that smile is real? Or is it something he uses to hide his fear of judgment, disapproval, and rejection? Do you think he wears that smile for people to like him, to accept him, to even love him?

Yes, the picture on the left was me five years ago. And although there is a noticeable difference between how I looked then compared to how I look today, my intention is not for you to focus on the external changes.

But rather, try to detect the internal differences …

So what is the fundamental difference between these two men?

The man on the left allowed others to control his life while the man on the right claimed responsibility for his own destiny and refused to let anything outside of him dictate his life.

The man on the right knows that his problems are the result of his choices, so he never blames anyone or anything outside of himself.

He takes responsibility for everything that goes on in his life. He knows that his ability to choose is his greatest freedom and greatest strength in life.

He knows that he can't always control what happens outside of him (e.g., the weather, the economy, other people), but he can always control his inner experience.

When he feels anger, fear, or sadness, he owns it. He knows it's his perspective that is creating the emotions, not the person or event outside of him.

Taking responsibility for your life is the secret to unlocking true freedom.

The man I was five years ago was far from free. He was living a life of indentured servitude, allowing everyone and everything outside of himself to control him.

Remember that today and every day you have a choice.

If there is anything we don't like about ourselves … if we are broke, overweight, lonely, miserable in our job, stressed out, unhappy, depressed, etc., we need to know two things:

We have chosen it.

Our choices got us there.

You can change almost anything in your life if you are aware of your choices and if your desire for a different reality is strong enough.

I share this story to illustrate my realization that the life I was living as an investment banker wasn't the life I wanted to create for myself. So I decided to surround myself and learn from some of the most successful, high-achieving entrepreneurs who had a life that I wanted.

At that point, I dedicated my life to studying entrepreneurs who were ultra-healthy, immensely wealthy, knowledgeable, vibrant, happy, and fulfilled in every area of their life. And as I started writing this book, I decided to interview these entrepreneurs and share exactly what they were doing to help others become more productive and successful. I decided to pull back the curtain and reveal what these badass entrepreneurs were doing differently, so you can create a similar quality of life.

Throughout this book I will share excerpts from these interviews. You can also download the full interviews for free by going to http://thefearlessmindsetbook.com.

Now I realize that getting fit in less time, doubling your income, and becoming unstoppable is a big promise! And I realize that you may struggle believing that you can do this. But if I was able to implement these habits and shift my mindset to create the life I'm living today, I promise you can too!

What You're Going to Learn

In order for you to become the badass you were born to be, you need to understand the essence of fear and what it means to have a fearless mindset.

Since fear affects everyone differently, I'm going to share with you in chapter 1 my story of being raised in chaos and how fear has affected my life.

In chapter 2, you'll learn how to distinguish the 2 types of fear that keep people from living the life of their dreams. You'll also learn how to overcome the 4 most common fears that separate the strong from the weak, the wealthy from the poor, and the lovers from the lonely.

In chapter 3, you'll learn why being fit gets you paid and the 7 most commonly held limiting beliefs, lies, and excuses most entrepreneurs make about fitness. You'll also discover a four-step framework called the fearless fitness journey, which can be applied to achieving goals in any area of your life.

Once you're armed with the mindset and habits necessary to get fit in less time, it's time you master the game of money and wealth creation. In chapter 4, you'll learn from some of the world's most successful entrepreneurs how to transform a financial scarcity mindset into a financial abundant mindset while experiencing the true essence of financial freedom. In addition you'll discover actionable wealth creation strategies that will immediately empower you to double, triple, even ten times your current income.

In chapter 5, you'll learn the ten non-negotiable beliefs of an unstoppable entrepreneur as well as actionable strategies to incorporate these beliefs into your own mindset so that you become unstoppable too.

Now that you've mastered your internal world, it's time to focus on your external world. In chapters 6 and 7, you will discover how to create a work environment that is optimal for peak performance. You'll also master the five-step process for demolishing the distractions in your environment so that you're hyper focused.

Have you ever experienced information overload? Well you may not realize this is one of the biggest deterrents from your productivity. So in chapter 7 you'll learn how to manage information overload by being purposeful and structured in your learning strategies.

Finally, in chapter 8, you'll discover how to instill "The Fearless Code" into your DNA and unleash the Fearless Mindset every single day.

Now that you know what to expect from this book, let's dive right in

Chapter 1:

Discovering How Your Fear Has Held You Back - *Chaos, fear and the (narrow) road to fearless living.*

In my experience coaching and mentoring some of the world's most successful entrepreneurs, I've discovered there is no such thing as being without fear. Even the most accomplished people experience fear, at least occasionally. What differentiates people who are living extraordinary lives from everyone else is that they don't let their fears stop them from taking action.

We are all affected by fear in one of three ways: (1) We are aware of our fears and are actively doing something to overcome them; (2) we are aware of our fears but are not doing anything to overcome them; or (3) we don't even know that fear is what is holding us back. This book addresses all three types of people affected by fear.

How many times do you find yourself frozen by fear? Your heart races; your breathing becomes shallow and fast. And soon you are paralyzed by trepidation.

Fear takes many forms, many of which I have personally experienced and overcome. I feared looking back on my life and discovering wasted opportunities or unrealized potential. I feared disappointing my family and losing their approval. I feared the unknown when starting out toward a new destination in my business.

Maybe you are a perfectionist and battle the fear of failure. Or you are afraid of losing your time freedom and limit yourself from reaching that next level of success in your business. Whatever brand of fear you are experiencing, the emotion can be debilitating.

But no matter how overwhelmed and paralyzed your fears are making you feel, you can break through to fearlessness. But before I go into how to begin taking steps toward this new way of being in chapter 2, "The Fearless Mindset," I want to share my story of how I was consumed by fear for twenty-five years.

Raised in Chaos

It's May 1995. At ten years old, I am terrified and alone. I don't know whom I could trust and seek guidance from for the most difficult conversation I am about to have in my life. Looking back at this moment, all I can remember is being consumed by fear.

I am sitting in a cold room with my mother, my grandparents, and an attorney. The smell of burnt coffee fills the air and the sound of a rusty furnace hums in the background. My mother is pale and looks exhausted. The glow of her face I once remembered and longed for is now gone. I want so badly to know what is going on in her mind, but we're both too afraid to look into each other's eyes.

I look to my grandparents to see their eyes carrying excruciating pain and sadness. I imagine their cascading thoughts as they reflect on how our family arrived in this room. Are they filled with regret? Are they relieved? The truth is, I'll never really know.

The attorney turns to me and says in a monotone

voice, "Peter, what is it you would like to tell your mother in this moment?" The lump in my throat grows with each passing second and I'm finding it hard to breath. My grandmother squeezes my hand in an effort to provide security and strength amidst the confusion and pain that encapsulates me.

My eyes begin to fill with tears. As I bite my tongue to keep from breaking down, I take one more deep breath, turn toward my mother, and say:

"Mom, I've decided to go live with Grandma and Grandpa since I no longer feel safe with you because of your alcoholism. Your alcoholism has consumed your life and I no longer feel loved by you. The only way my sister and I will feel comfortable living with you again is for you to go through rehab and choose, once and for all, to give up the bottle for your kids. It's your choice, Mom. If you want to be a part of our lives, you're going to have to give up drinking."

My mother runs across the room to embrace me one last time and we both break down weeping. This would be my mother's fourth time through rehab, and at this point in my life, I am doubtful that she will choose me and my sister over the bottle.

If there were one predominant emotion I remember from my childhood, it would have to be fear.

At ten years old, I didn't fully understand the impact that event in the courtroom would have on my life. But over the coming years I noticed, as I moved from place to place, that I had started to build these people-pleasing tendencies. Fearing that I was somehow deficient or not enough, I was driven to seek approval and validation from those around me. And as time went on, my fear and inner people-pleaser led to a life of inauthenticity.

Fast-forward to my early twenties as I finished college and started my career in investment banking. Although this was a very lucrative career, especially for somebody my age, I realized quickly that I wasn't passionate about what I was doing. I remember showing up to cocktail parties and meetings, pretending to be interested in the conversations around me, while all I wanted to do was scream. Before long, I realized that I was living a lie because I was afraid to leave the career that my family was so proud of.

And then one day I received a call from a family

member: "Peter, your dad has been rushed to the hospital, and you need to fly home immediately if you want to say good-bye." This was the fourth such call I got in five years.

My dad had literally given up on life and chose to drink himself to death.

I remember walking into the hospice and seeing my dad, a man who had once been my childhood hero, lying there emaciated in bed. I held his hand and asked, "Dad, why did you do this to yourself? Why did you do this to me?" He looked into my eyes and said, "Son, because I'm afraid."

My dad loved me so much, but he was consumed by the fear of not being good enough and of not living up to the expectations of his parents.

My father died at sixty years old because of his fears ... I was twenty-five.

After his death, I made a commitment to never let myself, a loved one, or anyone who comes into my life be controlled by fear. I committed to understanding, mastering, and overcoming my own fears by hiring mentors, attending classes, and reading books on the subject of fear. Facing my own fears and helping others break free of their fears led me to launch the Fearless Life Academy where I train high-achieving entrepreneurs to face their fears and live the life of their dreams.

This is a story I have told to audiences around the world, and with each telling I have learned to share more detail, presence, and heart.

I don't share this vulnerable story with you to seek sympathy; rather, I share it with you so that you understand how my life became consumed by fear.

Shortly after my father passed, I became introspective about the impact fear had on my life. I noticed that fear and limiting beliefs were the main constraints to changing anything I wasn't happy with in my life. And I became highly committed to uncovering and overcoming these fears by doing that which I feared.

Although fear still comes up from time to time, it never paralyzes me like it used to. I now recognize the fear, and act anyway. I have found the conviction within myself to do the very things I fear. I've learned that your ideal life is not something you just wish or hope for—it is something you make a choice to create for yourself.

My intention in writing this book is to help you overcome your fears so that you, too, can create the life of your dreams. In the next chapter, I will describe what it means to be truly fearless. You will discover exactly how to overcome the four most common fears that may be holding you back as well as the missing ingredient that instantly transforms your fear into excitement.

Chapter 2:

Developing Your Fearless Mindset – *Unlock the mystery behind the 2 types of fear and the 4 ways these fears show up in your life.*

What does it mean to be fearless? As I mentioned in chapter 1, being fearless is not the absence of fear. Fearlessness is about getting up one more time than you fall down. The more comfortable you are with the possibility of falling down, the more fearless you will be, and the easier your journey toward achieving your dreams will become.

I remember the first time I ever went skiing. I was twenty-four and I was terrified. There I was, in Vail, Colorado, going down the bunny slope without my poles, holding my instructor's hand. The moment I picked up a little speed my body tensed, my breathing became shallow and fast, and I lost my balance and fell. After doing this about a dozen times, I realized that falling wasn't actually so bad.

Eventually, I graduated from the bunny hill and took the ski lift to the top of my first green run. From the chair lift, I could see young children flying down black diamond slopes below me. While they weren't technically proficient skiers, it was evident that they had no fear. They were completely in flow, enjoying their rapid descent down the mountain.

When I accepted the likelihood of falling down, my body relaxed. And within a couple hours I had advanced from the green runs to the more challenging blue runs. On that day, I'm not sure I ever achieved the state of fearless flow I had witnessed in those young skiers charging down the black diamonds. But I do know that the less I feared falling down, the better I became at skiing.

When you think about it, the same is true with most of the challenges we face. The more comfortable you are with the possibility of falling down or failing, the more fearless you will be and the easier your journey will become.

Fear, then, is just a call to exercise courage. Without

fear, you cannot have courage. As my mentor Michael Hyatt says, "Courage is not the absence of fear—courage is the willingness to act in spite of your fear." So when I'm afraid, I've conditioned myself to walk right into my fears, rather than away from them.

If you create the habit of advancing toward your fears instead of retreating from them, your fear will dissipate. Most of the power of fear is in your mind. What you fear doesn't really exist. It's just an idea that looms because you are unwilling to face it. So the best way to defuse your fear is to step into it, right in the middle of it. And do the thing you are afraid to do.

So be courageous, today! Look the fear in the eye and shoot it down. Don't let it take you over. Don't let it win. Again, creating a fearless mindset doesn't mean all your fears will disappear. Creating a fearless mindset means that you will boldly move in the direction of your fears and reap the resulting benefits. Now lets explore the "2/4 Fear Factor" to unlock your fearless potential.

How to Distinguish the Two Types of Fear

During the writing of this book, I had the privilege of interviewing my mentor Jesse Elder on the subject of fear. Jesse is a Millionaire Mentor, an Improv Philosopher, and former mixed martial arts (MMA) fighter turned entrepreneur. He is the oldest of five, and has the unique distinction of never having taken a formal test of any kind. Without attending high school, college, or any other educational institution, Jesse's experience and perspective comes from a lifetime of focus on results, not theory. As an MMA fighter, Jesse experienced fear through face-to-face combat and developed a unique perspective on the two types of fear.

These two types of fear in life are rational and irrational fears. And Jesse believes the only difference from the "have's" and "have not's" is how they handle these two types of fear. The way one reacts to this distinction about fear separates the wealthy from the poor, the strong from the weak, and the lovers from the lonely:

Rational fears keep you alive, irrational fears keep you from living.

I've gone skydiving and found it to be one of the most

exhilarating experiences of my life. But the idea of jumping out of a plane without a parachute terrifies me. That's a rational fear that serves to keep me alive. Most fears, however, are irrational—they are not based on fact or reason—but we convince ourselves that our irrational fears are rational and make sense.

This is because both rational and irrational fears feel the same in our body. Our cortisol levels shoot up whether we're being chased by a lion or asking for the sale from a prospective client. Our heart begins to race, our breathing becomes shallow and fast, and our voice begins to quiver. The rational fear of a lion on the chase keeps us alive while the irrational fear of rejection keeps us from living.

The first time I was set to go skydiving, I felt an intense irrational fear. What made this fear irrational? For starters, I would be jumping tandem with an experienced skydiver who had over 16,000 jumps under his belt. Plus, statistically speaking, skydiving is safer than driving a car or flying a commercial airplane. Once I realized that my fear was irrational, I knew the only way to overcome it would be to go ahead and do that which I feared—in this case, jumping out of an airplane.

An Actionable Step to Overcoming Fear Now

So what is an irrational fear that you can work to overcome in your life? As a practical step, think of something you are afraid of that's an irrational fear. It should be something that's not going to cause you physical harm, drain your bank account, or destroy your relationship.

The most common irrational fears include the fear of failure, the fear of rejection or disapproval, the fear of the unknown, and the fear of financial poverty.

Let's start by imagining, for example, that you are scheduled to give a presentation to a large group of people and you have a tremendous fear of public speaking. To determine whether this fear is rational or irrational, you could ask yourself some simple questions: Do you believe that this fear is keeping you alive or preventing you from fully living? What is the chance you will actually die in the process of public speaking? Almost zero. So looking at that fear again, you recognize that it is an irrational fear. It works to prevent you from living, rather than serving the purpose of keeping you alive.

Once you have determined your fear is irrational, you can make the commitment to overcome it today by doing the thing you fear. Now this action needs to do something that's a radical shock to your comfort zone. It needs to make your knees shake, your palms sweat, and put your heart in your throat. Going back to our example of the irrational fear of public speaking, your action step might be to join a local public speaking group like Toastmasters so that you can start giving speeches to the group to overcome your fear.

After you take this action step, you'll go to bed tonight knowing that you have done something different. And you will wake up tomorrow with a new past. After repeating this new behavior of doing the thing you fear over a couple weeks, it will become a habit. More important, you will realize that the thing you are afraid of is an illusion. It does not exist.

Here's a practical tactic that Jesse Elder challenged me to do:

Call somebody you've been holding a grudge against for years. Call them up and say: "Hey, it's me. The reason I'm calling you is because I've been thinking about how angry I've been at you. And then I realized that by being angry at you, it's like I'm drinking poison and waiting for you to die. So, I'm calling you right now to tell you that I was angry but I'm not anymore. I forgive you. You did the best you could with what you had at the moment, and so did I. And we are just two people making our way through this world. I don't require anything from you. I don't need anything from you. I just want to tell you that I forgive you. So have a great life!"

The power that you will unleash by facing that fear and making that single phone call will be the wind that launches your ship to the next destination. So, are your knees shaky? Are your palms sweaty? Is your heart in your throat? Good! Then that's the thing you need to do, today. If you don't have this kind of fear to get over, think of a different kind of irrational fear that may be holding you back and then take an action step today. Now that you understand the difference between rational and irrational fears, it's time to transform your fear into excitement.

Fear and Excitement Are the Same Emotion

Fear and excitement are almost the same exact

emotion because both release similar chemicals and hormones in the body.

To illustrate this point, imagine that you're on a roller coaster that you've never been on before. As your cart pulls away from the gate, you start thinking to yourself, "Oh my gosh, I don't know how this is going to look. I don't know how extreme the drop is on the other side of this peak. I don't know where the curves are going to bring me and what's at the end of the roller coaster."

You can wonder about these thoughts with two different energies: a fearful energy or an excited energy.

A fearful energy creates constriction in your body. Your breath becomes shallow. You feel nervous, anxious, and worried about the unknown. On the other hand, you may choose to approach these same questions with excitement and curiosity. You welcome the feelings arising in your body and the unknown that lies ahead.

One of the most profound pieces of wisdom I've ever heard comes from Fritz Perl, the psychiatrist and founder of Gestalt therapy. He said, "Fear is excitement without the breath." This means that the same mechanisms that produce excitement also produce fear, and any fear can be transformed into excitement by breathing fully into it. On the other hand, excitement immediately turns into fear if we hold our breath. When feeling fear, most of us try to get rid of it by denying or ignoring it. The problem is that we use holding our breath as a physical tool of denial.

The reality is that the less breath you feed your fear, the bigger your fear becomes. The best advice I can give you is to take big, deep breaths when you feel fear. You must feel the fear instead of pretending it's not there. So the next time you experience fear, try breathing into it and consciously turn it into excitement.

How to Overcome the Four Most Common Fears

I can preach all day that fear is an illusion, but the reality is that it doesn't feel like an illusion when you're consumed by that fear.

So now that we've defined the difference between

rational and irrational fears, and explained that fear can be a good thing, I'm going to dive deep into the four most common fears that hold us back from achieving our dreams. You'll recall that these were all listed earlier as irrational fears.

Fear of Failure

"The greatest mistake you can make in life, is to continually be afraid you will make one."

—*Elbert Hubbard*

The fear of failure can be the most debilitating fear of all because it restricts action, and action is the foundational ingredient to achieving anything you want in life.

Many people let their fear of failure mask itself as procrastination. In other words, they never get started on the task they're afraid of failing at. So how do you overcome this debilitating fear? I'm going to share a story with you about a friend who overcame devastating failures to win at the game of life.

From Super Bowl Winner to Broke

From Super Bowl winner to broke, from mortgage empire to bankruptcy, Setema Gali Jr. has overcome devastating failures to win at the game of life. As a focused and determined athlete, Setema worked his way through five shoulder surgeries and multiple concussions to become a defensive captain and one of the top collegiate football players in the country.

His dedication and perseverance to football paid off. After graduating from Brigham Young, he embarked on his professional sports career with the New England Patriots. After winning Super Bowl thirty-six and retiring with a serious back injury, Setema found himself living in his mom's basement. His possessions included a college degree, a Super Bowl ring, and zero dollars in his bank account. But Setema wasn't down or out. He relied on the same work ethic and skills that had made him a champion on the field and now applied them off the field.

In time, Setema built up a mortgage–real estate empire that brought in a healthy multiple six-figure monthly income. Life was amazing. He also married his best friend and the couple had a healthy baby boy. Setema thought his challenging days were over.

Then in 2008, the mortgage industry collapsed, and with it went Setema's four years of hard work. He lost everything, including ten homes and four cars. Brought back to zero once again, Setema began questioning whether life was worth living.

How bad did things get?

He sold his wife's wedding ring and most of their possessions just to pay the bills. He also resorted to selling his Super Bowl ring to survive the financial onslaught brought on by the mortgage bubble. Although his back was definitely against the wall, Setema would not quit. Instead, he reclaimed his power and certainty, this time through the sheer hard work of knocking on doors as a door-to-door salesman.

It was during this time of pounding the pavement in the hot humid weather of the Deep South that Setema recommitted to finding the keys to loving life no matter what. While recruiting, building, and growing his new business, Setema discovered and re-created his map for loving life—no matter the circumstances, no matter the situation, no matter what was going on in business or in his personal life.

Setema attributes his ability to bounce back after such devastating failures to the driving force he calls his "why" or purpose. He suggests embracing the struggle rather than avoiding it. And today, he mentors professional athletes to create personal road maps of success, love and happiness..

═══════════════════════════════════════

So instead of fearing failure and doing everything in your power to avoid it, consider failing as quickly and as often as possible, knowing that the path to success is paved by experiencing failure. And if the fear of failure begins creeping back into your consciousness, remember Setema's story and how he overcame not just the fear of failure but actual failure—including losses so profound he was forced to sell his Super Bowl ring and begin knocking doors as a door-to-door salesman—to create an extraordinary life for himself and his family.

Fear of Rejection/Disapproval

The fear of rejection/disapproval is generally ingrained in us at a very young age. It often starts with being criticized by our parents, the people we most want approval from. Whether it's for the way we throw a baseball or the A+ we received on our report card, we are highly dependent at a young age for approval and validation from our parents and other loved ones.

So what happens when we lose that game or get a bad grade on our report card? We start to endure criticism from our parents. And soon we realize that criticism doesn't feel good and is something to be avoided at almost any cost. While some might argue that trying to avoid criticism and live up to our parents' or others' high standards or expectations is actually a positive, the problem is that living in fear of rejection/disapproval robs us of our initiative, destroys our power of imagination, limits our individuality, and takes away our self-reliance.

The fastest way to overcome this fear is to first become aware of when you are seeking approval or validation. Whether from a parent, a mentor, a client, or friend, you must explore why you want approval from this person. What does their approval provide to you? Once you uncover this connection, it's easier to let go of this need and become unaffected by rejection or disapproval. Stop and consider what your life would look like if you had no fear of rejection. How would you feel and act on a day-to-day basis? Overcoming this one fear allows you to live your life on your terms regardless of what others may think.

Fear of the Unknown

When starting out as an entrepreneur, clarity is often a result not a prerequisite. If I waited until I had a crystal clear vision before launching my business, I wouldn't have a business right now. I would be sitting on the sidelines reading books, listening to audio programs, and attending seminars.

All of these things are good to do, as long as you're also taking massive action toward building your business.

I didn't know exactly whom I was going to coach or what my message was going to be when I launched my coaching business. But I became ruthlessly committed to creating and communicating content with the marketplace. Over time, my message became clear, and the vision for my business became tangible.

Your fears, doubts, and limiting beliefs of what lies ahead never disappear, so waiting for them to vanish will leave you waiting a long time. Commit to taking the action necessary today to get one step further in your business and your life.

Fear of Financial Poverty

Fear of financial poverty is a state of mind, nothing else! In chapter 4, "Double Your Income," I will describe in detail exactly what creates a poverty mindset and how you can transform a mindset of financial scarcity into a mindset of financial abundance. Right now, I want to share an excerpt from Napoleon Hill's book Think & Grow Rich that aptly expresses the devastating impact that the fear of financial poverty has on one's life:

> This fear of poverty paralyzes the faculty of reason, destroys the faculty of imagination, kills off self-reliance, undermines enthusiasm, discourages initiative, leads to uncertainty of purpose, encourages procrastination, wipes out enthusiasm and makes self-control an impossibility. It takes

the charm from one's personality, destroys the possibility of accurate thinking, diverts concentration of effort, it masters persistence, turns the will-power into nothingness, destroys ambition, beclouds the memory and invites failure in every conceivable form; it kills love and assassinates the finer emotions of the heart, discourages friendship and invites disaster in a hundred forms, leads to sleeplessness, misery and unhappiness—and all this despite the obvious truth that we live in a world of over-abundance of everything the heart could desire, with nothing standing between us and our desires, excepting lack of a definite purpose.

What I know to be true from my own life experience and from interviewing some of the world's most successful entrepreneurs is that wealth is not a number; wealth is a feeling. We're conditioned by society to want the fast car, nice suits, and big mansion. Yet what we really want are the feelings that we think those possessions will make us feel: worthiness, significance, powerful, love, respect.

The fastest way to overcome the fear of financial poverty is by appreciating all the resources you already have in your life. By creating a need-free appreciation of money, you will develop a sense of peace around creating wealth. When you are operating from a place of peaceful appreciation, you create far more wealth than when you operate from neediness or obligation. This topic will be addressed in much greater detail in chapter 4, "Double Your Income."

Now that you're aware of the four most common fears holding entrepreneurs back from their dreams, let's dive into mindset shifts and actionable strategies to help you accomplish success in an area of life you have probably been neglecting – your physical health and fitness. Read on to learn how to get fit, even if you have no time for fitness.

Chapter 3:

Getting Fit in Less Time – *How to banish the 7 lies holding you back and embrace the simple fitness journey that will set you free to achieve anything you want in ANY area of life.*

The Fearless Fitness Framework is a blueprint that all fearlessly fit entrepreneurs live by. It is a framework that is rooted in one powerful yet simple statement:

Being fit gets you paid!

As we discussed previously, most entrepreneurs' primary focus is growing their business so that they make more money. The problem is that by focusing solely on their business, they neglect the areas of their life that give them the power to produce at their highest potential. Since being fit gets you paid, neglecting your health and fitness limits your energy, focus, and confidence required to grow your business and double, triple, or even increase your income tenfold.

By prioritizing your fitness through daily non-negotiable fitness habits, you wake up each day with more energy, focus, and confidence to crush your business goals.

This concept defines the Fearlessly Fit Entrepreneur: An entrepreneur who is crushing it in business while being in amazing shape, having deeply connected relationships with their family, and living a life of purpose. This is the framework that's going to be emphasized throughout this book. So if you want to double your income, and if you want to create a badass life, you need to be in great shape, period.

Now you may be thinking to yourself as you read this, "Who cares about fitness if I'm making more money than I ever thought imaginable?" Well, I personally know many incredibly wealthy entrepreneurs who are miserable with their lives. And the reason they're miserable is that they don't have the level of physical fitness required to enjoy life's greatest adventures.

Imagine being a billionaire who can travel the world in luxury, but you don't have the level of fitness required to climb the Great Pyramids or hike the Inca trail. Picture having the financial freedom to pursue life's greatest adventures, but you lack the strength and stamina to fully experience them. By neglecting their health in favor of focusing solely on making more money, this is the sad reality awaiting most entrepreneurs who achieve this level of success.

How Being Fit Gets You Paid

Yes, being healthy and fit so you can enjoy the pleasures and adventures made possible by financial success makes sense, but why exactly does being fit get you paid? Well, let me share with you three principles that will permanently change the way you view fitness.

Productivity Power Principle
The first principle is called the Productivity Power Principle. It states that your energy and focus directly impact your productivity, and as your productivity increases, you become more powerful in every area of your life.

For example, if you wake up groggy and find yourself

reaching for coffee or energy drinks throughout the day, then you are experiencing an energy drain that is limiting your productivity. This limited productivity is negatively impacting your personal power to show up confidently with your clients and prospects. And the primary root cause of limited energy is lack of exercise.

Starting your day with intense exercise creates a domino effect on every other area of your life. Through exercising, you gain unstoppable energy that makes you feel confident about conquering your biggest obstacles and adversities. And, most important, when you feel more powerful, you act decisively and courageously by doing the things you might otherwise be afraid to do in your business.

This doesn't mean you no longer feel fear. Rather, it means that you are cultivating courage to do the things you fear. And when you start doing the things you fear in business, your income soars.

A Case Study on How Fitness Impacts Fear

I'm sitting in the lobby of Paradise Point Resort in sunny San Diego with the smell of saltwater in the air, the sound of joyful tourists enjoying their vacations, and world-renowned speaker Sean Stephenson (www.seanstephenson.com) sitting across from me.

If there were one person in the world who has had to overcome debilitating fears to become a successful entrepreneur, it would be Sean.

When Sean was born, doctors predicted he would not survive because of a rare bone disorder that stunted his growth and made his bones extremely fragile. His body was so fragile, he could fracture a rib from just sneezing. By the time he was eighteen years old, he had over 200 fractures in his body. Let me say that again: 200 fractures!

So as I sit down to interview this man who has been called a three-foot giant, Sean begins to tell me how his commitment to fitness has empowered him to face his greatest fears …

Sean: Fitness has helped with my fears because it taps into something primal. When you are exercising, burning calories, and sweating, you hit a space inside your mind that triggers something animalistic and makes you realize that you're dangerous. You can do some damage.

It's not that you would want to, but rather you have a knowing that your body is powerful. And that makes you think you are capable of really shaking the mountains in your business and in your life.

Whenever I'm fearful, I turn to the things that give me the upper hand on my fears. I might reach out for mentorship. I might reach out for good coaches. And I might reach out for my animalistic triggers by going to the gym.

Rather than running from your fears, you become so powerful that your fears start to fear you. You see, I'm no less fearful than you. I have multiple business projects coming up that I have all kinds of fears around.

But I tell myself, "I'm doing this whether the fear is there or not." I don't care. I'm not going to wait for the fear to be gone to do something. In life, you have to do the things that you fear so that you no longer fear them.

I like what Eleanor Roosevelt said, which is: "In life,

you must do the things that you think you can't do." And if you do the things you think you can't do, you will constantly be breaking records. You will constantly be striving for more and better. You will constantly be growing out of your comfort zone and making an impact.

The Time-Freedom Formula

"Time is the coin of your life. It is the only coin you have, and only you can determine how it will be spent."

—*Carl Sandburg*

At the end of our lives when we're on our deathbed, we're not going to be thinking about the amount of money that we wish we made. We're going to be reflecting on how well we used the limited time we had on this earth.

We all have twenty-four hours in a day. No one has more or less than that. So the question isn't, How do I create more time? That's simply impossible. The question is, How do I get more done in less time? Through my experience coaching high-achieving entrepreneurs, I've discovered the number one reason they don't prioritize their fitness is their belief that they are too busy and don't have enough time.

The Time-Freedom Formula illustrates that you can actually get more done in less time by prioritizing fitness. Now how is it possible to get more done by investing your limited time into fitness? When you commit to exercising every single day you skyrocket your energy, focus, and confidence and this empowers you to get more done in less time. When you start your day with an intense workout, you are able to think more clearly and take more action. When you are in a high-energy, action-oriented state, you can accomplish in four hours what normally takes you eight hours to complete.

This shift of perspective about the relationship between fitness and time will forever transform your productivity and expand your capacity to make more money than you ever dreamed.

The Decisive Action Principle

"Every noteworthy achievement the world has ever seen was born with a single thought; and every great man who ever lived has been a man of decision."

—Raymond Barker

The third principle that supports the belief that being fit gets you paid is the Decisive Action Principle.

I've been on a mission to maximize human potential and accelerate human achievement for as long as I can remember. As early as the eighth grade, I was reading business and self-help books to better myself. Over the years, I've attended countless seminars and invested tens of thousands of dollars in my own personal development. I've sought out some of the most incredible human beings to mentor me in different areas of my life so that I could shorten the learning curve and start seeing results faster.

I don't say this to brag or seek praise. Rather, I'm sharing this so you understand that I'm speaking from experience rather than from just theory.

So if you're anything like me, searching for the secret knowledge that has eluded you, I'll open up the curtain for you to see the truth behind the "magic" of accelerating your results to create time freedom …

The difference between entrepreneurs who are slaves to time and entrepreneurs who have freedom from time comes down to one simple principle—decisive action.

For the majority of my life, I've been neutralized by my habit of "needing" every last piece of sacred information before allowing myself to take action. This form of self-indoctrination, and lack of trust in my own ability, left me a slave to time.

As I look at the entrepreneurs who have created time freedom, I realize they have not achieved this because they have better information than I have. It's not because they think positively and put out a fuzzy intention, and the Universe magically grants their every wish. No, they have time freedom for the simple reason that they take decisive action. Here's how Dusan Djukich, Co-Founder of Corporate Reinvention Associates, describes what it means to act decisively:

> Effective people don't focus on their concerns. They simply act decisively. Fear or no fear. They know that all results come out of decisive action. So rather than looking for the courage, or the strength, or "enough time" to do something important,

they forget all that. It's too mentally exhausting to work on all that. So they just drop the preconditions. They know from experience that getting from A to B is always about doing the next required action.

Can you relate to this as a high-achieving entrepreneur? I've sure experienced my most productive days when I'm acting decisively in every area of my life.

The reality is that you don't need discipline to take action. You don't need confidence to take action. And you sure as hell don't need to be without fear to take action. You simply need to take responsibility for your actions by doing what you should do, when you should do it, whether you feel like it or not.

This is the primary reason I work with a coach— so that I'm held accountable for doing what I say I'm going to do every single week, regardless of whether I feel like it or not.

So where in your life are you avoiding decisive action? Where in your life are you procrastinating and making excuses? I want you to consider how your life would be different if you started acting decisively today. What would happen to your business? How would this new commitment affect your health and fitness? How could this increase the trust and intimacy in your love relationship?

Making a commitment to your fitness is the quickest way to start acting decisively. When you commit to a daily fitness habit, such as sweating every single day, you start cultivating a more powerful inner state. And as you build this inner strength, outer decisiveness naturally follows.

The more decisive you are, the more you get done in less time. You no longer waste hours and hours mentally pontificating and wavering on a decision. You decide swiftly and act with certainty, freeing you from being a slave to time. What's more, this new mode of decisive action produces more income in your business than you ever thought imaginable.

Now that you're aware of the three principles establishing why being fit gets you paid, let's explore the seven most common excuses, lies, and myths holding entrepreneurs back from committing to their health and fitness.

The Fearless Fitness Lies

We all know what needs to be done to get fit. At the end of the day, it really is simple: exercise more and eat better. So why do so few people actually reach their vision for their ideal health and fitness? It's not a lack of information. We are inundated with exercise tips and fly-by-night diets on every media source you can imagine. If anything, there is too much information available, leading many to be confused about which direction to take.

So rather than adding to your confusion by offering more exercise and nutrition advice, which is only temporarily treating the surface-level symptoms, I'm going to instead address the root cause of the fitness crisis facing not just entrepreneurs but human beings in general. The problem is that the game of health and fitness is lost before it even begins.

No matter its quality, fitness and nutrition information is useless if you don't have the right mindset to act on that information. So in this next section, I'm going to address the limiting beliefs that you've likely developed and the lies society has told you about your health and fitness. The fitness industry has been marketing false promises and lies in order to convince you to spend more money. Oftentimes, your family, friends, and the environments around you have contributed to those lies, forming the limiting beliefs that have ultimately held you back from taking effective action.

Before I detail the actionable strategies that will support you in building lasting fitness and nutrition habits, let's look at the commonly held limiting beliefs, lies, and excuses around fitness.

Lie #1: Exercise doesn't produce money in my business.

The truth is exercise actually gives you the energy, the clarity of thought, and the stamina to push through your projects, create more value for your clients, and make more money than you ever imagined in your business.

You see, most entrepreneurs are so focused on their business that they neglect every other area of their life, especially their fitness. Can you relate to that?

You wake up exhausted in the morning and start your day by guzzling down coffee. Then 2 p.m. hits and you're drained again, so you start consuming energy drinks and other stimulants. This leads to consistent energy crashes throughout the remainder of your day, which have to be mitigated with additional stimulants. When you show up with limited energy and focus, you aren't able to produce at your highest potential in your business.

Consider this statement: being healthy and fit will lead to all the results you want in your business. This is the secret connection that very few entrepreneurs understand. Those who do often go on to become fearlessly fit entrepreneurs and differentiate themselves from their counterparts, the overwhelmed, exhausted entrepreneur.

You see, being in the best shape of your life is what gets you paid. It gives you certainty. It promotes confidence. When you feel more certain and confident, you show up in front of your clients and know that you can create the most value for them, resulting in more business and more income.

It is your duty and your obligation to prioritize your health and fitness. When you have that foundation—when you wake up and know what your daily actions and habits are, and you start your day with exercise—it affects every other area of your life. Putting your body first will impact and improve everything else you encounter in your day, especially when it comes to your business.

[Success Story From Dean Grafos]
From: Dean Grafos
To: Peter Scott IV
Subject: My Business Had Its Best Month Ever

When I first met Peter I already had a successful business, a good workout and overall health regimen, and a happy marriage. I was also one year into my spiritual journey, trying to find a happier and more focused existence.

I felt like I had all the tools needed to accomplish this goal, but just needed the right method of putting everything in place.

When I spoke to Peter, I realized right away that he

was the person to help me put it all together.

I felt an instant connection to his passion for his business and his fitness, and admired the way he was 100% present and connected during our conversation.

What I soon realized was that I did NOT have the tools needed to facilitate my spiritual journey in any effective or meaningful way, my health regimen was less than 50% of my capabilities, and my family life was not nearly as happy as it could be. In fact, my family life desperately needed help.

In the first month I worked with Peter, I completed approximately 50% of the baseline goals I had set for myself. Even at a 50% effort, I already experienced significant change in ALL aspects of my life …

My business profits increased, I was working out more, my family was getting more connected, and I felt more positive and happier in general.

Given these gains, I went all in and committed 100% effort to month two. The results were astonishing …

It was by far the most productive month I had ever

had in my life up to that point. Every aspect of my life was significantly better.

My business had its best month ever, my workouts were through the roof, I was eating healthier than ever, I felt stronger than ever, and I was starting to experience a peace and calmness in my life that was completely foreign to me.

The third month I decided to dedicate even more effort toward my family life and spirituality. I was amazed to find that by the end, my connection to my wife was stronger than ever.

I was able to clearly see a huge difference from just 90 days earlier, and see that this was just the beginning.

I got a glimpse into how awesome life COULD be. This is after 13 years of marriage!

I also noticed that the connection with my daughter also improved, and SHE was noticing the changes in ME. She even told me, "Daddy you seem really happy." She had never said anything like that to me before and it made me so proud of my decision to fully commit to changing my life.

In just 90 days every aspect of my life improved in very significant ways and I now have a Life-System to utilize as I continue on my journey.

Peter was (and continues to be) very inspiring to work with. He was there for me ANY time I needed him, and always had the right words to keep me focused, positive, and on track.

He really listened to my issues and always had a solution.

What I admire most about him is the way he lives his own life with integrity. He is 100% committed to living the lifestyle he promotes.

I strongly encourage ANYONE seeking a better life to commit 100% to hiring Peter as your mentor and coach.

I promise you …

Your life will change!

Lie #2: The solution I want is a magic pill, product, or lotion.

Let me bust a myth that we've all been brainwashed to believe:

There is no such thing as results without effort!

We've been marketed get-rich-quick schemes and magic diet pills our entire lives. The truth is we're not missing a magic pill. We're not missing the knowledge of what to do. What's missing is our own commitment to doing the work required to achieve the results we want.

You see, until we make that commitment, it doesn't matter how many products we buy off of late-night infomercials. If we're not clear on exactly what we want and why we have a burning desire to achieve that result, the exercise program or diet we start will not be sustainable. We won't take the actions required to achieve the results we want until we get crystal clear on our vision and purpose.

Remember, if you're not prioritizing your health and fitness; if you're not doing the daily habits and rituals you need to skyrocket your energy, focus, and confidence; your business will suffer.

One of my first coaching clients had a massive breakthrough when he finally accepted that there is no such thing as results without effort. Once he accepted this fact and stopped searching for magic diet pills, products, or lotions, he made a permanent lifestyle change that produced results he didn't know he had the potential to achieve.

Steve hired me as his coach when he weighed 330 pounds. He was sad, depressed, and felt alone. Although Steve ran a successful business, he noticed his revenue potential was limited by his lack of energy and the sheer physical pain he was in. Over time, Steve's pain became so excruciating that his doctor prescribed him painkillers. The painkillers were effective in providing temporary relief, but they were only masking his symptoms—they were not solving the problem at the root of his pain.

During one of our coaching calls, he admitted that he became addicted to prescription painkillers and it was affecting his ability to think clearly and focus at work. He had tried to lose weight multiple times over the years, hiring multiple personal trainers who started him on aggressive fitness routines, which only led him to quit days later.

So instead of proposing a radical diet and fitness routine that could overtax his body and lead to yet another failure, I helped him create a plan of simple daily health. He started with short daily walks to get his body in motion and added a daily green smoothie to his nutrition plan.

Within a couple weeks he started feeling better about himself and he started to shed some weight. After a month, Steve started limiting the prescription painkillers he was taking, which improved his clarity of thought and focus.

Today, Steve is completely off of prescription painkillers. He is exercising consistently and eating healthier. These small changes led him to take responsibility for his health, rather than handing it over to somebody else to fix.

Steve had been on the path toward an early death, but

rather than remain a victim, he chose to take responsibility for his health and made small changes that turned into a permanent lifestyle.

Now this wasn't easy for Steve. But by breaking down his goals into smaller benchmarks and committing to daily habits, he was able to lose significant weight and break his reliance on prescription painkillers.

So where do you need to create habits in your life to help you get off of your "prescription drugs"—a metaphor for anything you've become reliant on to mask your pain. It could be drinking, smoking, pornography, or any other outlet you use to escape reality.

Your life is limited and tomorrow isn't promised. Ask yourself why you would choose to escape your reality when you only have a limited amount of time left. I don't say this to be morbid; I say this to be real. You are responsible for your current quality of life and it is in your power to make changes to create the new reality that you desire.

Rather than seeking that next magic diet pill or get-rich-quick scheme, make the commitment to yourself to do the work. It won't be easy, but I promise you it will be worth it.

Lie #3: My genetics are the reason I'm not fit.

When we blame our genetics for our lack of fitness, we're choosing to be victims. We're neglecting our responsibility and casting the blame on something we cannot control. Earlier I shared with you an interview I did with my best friend, Sean Stephenson, a man born with a disorder that made his bones extremely fragile.

Despite the physical challenges he has faced his entire life, he's taken a stand for a quality of life that has reached millions of people around the world, including Sir Richard Branson, President Clinton, and His Holiness the 14th Dalai Lama.

He's appeared on everything from The Oprah Show to Youtube videos with millions of views. The Biography Channel even did an hour-long feature on his life called 3 Foot Giant.

His message has been heard at live events in more than fifteen countries and forty-seven states over the past sixteen years. His latest book, Get Off Your But, swept through the United States and was released in over a half dozen languages around the world.

So how in the world was Sean able to do this? you ask.

Sean became powerful inside before he was powerful outside. He consciously cultivates character traits like self-responsibility, determination, and emotional fortitude to handle the daily adversities he faces. He exercises and lifts weights every single day, and he's made the commitment and taken the stand in his life to not be a victim and blame his genetics.

I share Sean's story because, like many others, you may have blamed your genetics for the current reality of your health and fitness. You may come from a family that's overweight. You may feel like you're gaining weight whenever you look at food. Whatever the circumstances that led you to where you are today, you can choose a different reality. You can choose to make a permanent lifestyle change through your daily actions and habits. When we let go of our story about genetics, we transition from being the victim we've always been to the badass we were born to be.

Lie #4: I don't have time to work out.

The truth is, we don't have spare time to work out, so we must create time to work out. I'm going to share a story with you about one of the most successful and busiest entrepreneurs on the planet. You may have heard of him, a billionaire entrepreneur named Richard Branson.

During an interview, Branson was once asked, "Richard, what is the secret to your success?" Here is the answer he gave: "I exercise every single day." Think about how busy Richard Branson must be and yet he has still made the commitment to work out every day.

He probably doesn't "have the time" to exercise, but he recognizes the connection between his fitness and his business success.

When it comes to fitness, the biggest excuse holding entrepreneurs back is the limiting belief that they should devote more of their time and energy to their business. The reality is that when we neglect our health and fitness, our business suffers. My own experience confirms this.

When I look back at my coaching business, the months when I'm crushing it financially and earning the most are the same months that I'm crushing it in my fitness. I'm in motion and sweating every single day. Between CrossFit, yoga, weight training, running, surfing, and rock climbing, I'm exercising every day.

Let's be clear: Following a daily exercise regimen doesn't require that you invest one to two hours a day to your fitness. There are days when I have early morning commitments, so instead of carving out ninety minutes to go surfing, I go for a quick fifteen-minute run. My commitment is to sustain my fitness habit by being in motion every single day, not to dedicate a set amount of time to a strict routine. Imagine what your life would look like if you made this same commitment. Imagine how energized and powerful you would feel. Imagine how this would impact your love life or your relationship with your children. Give yourself permission to unlock your greatest business—and life—potential by making this commitment today.

Lie #5: Fitness is too boring.

The truth is, fitness can be incredibly fun if you clarify

what fun fitness looks like to you. The problem is that few people ever take the time to find out what they actually enjoy about fitness to make it fun. Instead they blindly follow some routine that a personal trainer hands them, even if they find it incredibly boring. Sure, they may stay committed for a couple weeks after making a significant financial investment, or through their willpower or self-discipline, but is this really sustainable in the long term?

Have you ever had an experience like this? You walk into a gym, find a personal trainer, and say, "I'd like to lose twenty pounds. What do I do?" What is the typical trainer's response? He or she hands you a one-size-fits-all routine and says, "Okay. Go run on a treadmill. If you want to lose twenty pounds, just go run on a treadmill."

If you don't enjoy running on a treadmill, no matter how great the results may be, you're never going to follow through with it. You're never going to take the action necessary that will make a significant improvement in your health and fitness. Before you start something else by default, get clear on what you enjoy about fitness.

I never run on a treadmill because it's incredibly boring to me. I would rather watch paint dry. I love activities that involve being outside. I love variety and working out with friends. So I've created an exercise routine that involves a mixture of activities—CrossFit, yoga, surfing, rock climbing, running, tennis, and beach volleyball. All these forms of exercise are radically different from one another and I'm constantly switching it up week to week. With this level of variety, there's nothing boring about my fitness routine.

I struggled with this for years, and it's something you may be struggling with too. So I challenge you to stop going through life on autopilot and take the time to slow down and answer this question, "What could I really enjoy about fitness?"

Lie #6: I've tried everything and nothing works.

In reality, if you've tried everything, you haven't stayed committed to one thing long enough to see results. The reason I know this is because this was my personal journey. I would start exercise routine after exercise routine, committing to each one for just thirty days. But when I didn't get the results I wanted in that limited timeframe, I would give up, quit, and go find the next exercise routine or diet.

If you think you've tried everything, you may need to make longer commitments. Remember, we're not in this for a quick fix. There is no such thing as results without effort. Instead, consider making a permanent and profound lifestyle change: a new way of living from this day forth through the rest of your life. In doing so, you'll also inspire your partner or spouse, your children, your friends, your business partners, and your clients to make health and fitness a priority in their lives as well.

Lie #7: I can do this alone.

Listen, I get it. As a fearlessly fit entrepreneur, you may be inclined to try to take responsibility for your life and strive for your goals on your own. But there's a certain point when you're going to need guidance. You're going to need someone to hold you accountable. And you're going to need to associate with others who are on this same journey. This is the entire purpose of the Fearless Life Academy: to support overworked entrepreneurs to create a fearless mindset so they get fit in less time, double their income, and become unstoppable.

Consider finding a mentor and joining a mastermind group of others who are committed to creating daily habits and rituals to grow their businesses and increase their earnings. What would happen if you weren't alone? What would happen if you had a mentor and a group to check in with every single week? How would your results change?

Jason came to the Fearless Life Academy with the desire to create a life that he loved. He wanted to be healthy, wealthy, knowledgeable, vibrant, and happy. One of Jason's biggest challenges was his addiction to smoking and alcohol.

The problem was that he felt a tremendous amount of peer pressure from his friends who spent most of their time partying at bars and clubs. Jason wanted to create meaningful and deep relationships with people who were health conscious, active, and passionate about their personal growth. But by associating himself with his current group of friends, he found himself at the bars every weekend. And once he had a few drinks, he ended up smoking again.

Jason knew this behavior was bad for him. He knew

that it would eventually cause cancer and lead to an early death. But he still struggled with stopping his use. So, instead of having him attempt to quit smoking overnight, I challenged him to commit to daily fitness and nutrition habits, meditation practices, and personal development reading that would help him feel better about his life.

Jason agreed, and as he started developing these new habits and creating a life he loved, he began meeting more like-minded people at events and seminars he attended. And since he found himself around more health-conscious people, he began limiting his smoking and drinking more and more until one day he was able to completely quit the most challenging addiction of his life.

Another challenge Jason was facing was that of moving on from a devastating breakup. He was approaching forty and felt that he had just lost the love of his life. Yet the problem causing his sadness and depression wasn't the actual breakup; it was the fact the he was seeking love and validation outside of himself.

This lack of self-love led Jason to constantly seek

validation from women. Through this approval seeking, he created shallow and meaningless relationships. Can you relate to this at all? I know there was a time in my life when I sought this kind of validation and approval. I remember doing things I wouldn't normally do in order to win the love of a woman. And then one day I made it my mission to create a life that I loved: a life where I didn't need approval or validation from anyone outside of myself.

When Jason was smoking, drinking, and having casual sex with women who didn't mean anything to him, he was searching for love and acceptance. But now, working with a group of other entrepreneurs and making himself accountable to them, he turned off that path and onto one that allowed him to create a life that he loved. A life filled with deep, meaningful relationships. A life built on growth, passion, and self-love. Through his new belief in himself and through this process, he was able to move on from a very painful breakup and become more vibrant, grounded, and happy.

This is what I know is possible for you. This is true whether you can relate to Dean, struggling to break through your revenue limits; or Steve, significantly overweight and addicted to painkillers; or Jason, lacking self-love, self-reliance, and escaping your life through drugs and alcohol.

Whoever you are and no matter your situation, you have a choice. You have the ability to create the life that you want. It is your moral obligation and duty to do so. No one is going to hand it to you. It takes commitment. It takes clarity. And it takes a fearless dedication to doing what needs to be done so that you create the life of your dreams.

The Fearless Fitness Journey

The fearless fitness journey is a four-step process that will get you from where you are today in your body—stressed, overwhelmed, and feeling guilty about neglecting your fitness— to the vision you want to achieve: where you have more energy, greater focus, higher productivity, and a body that commands respect.

You can use this four-step process to achieve goals in any area of your life. We're going to go through this entire process right now because your health and fitness is the foundation to everything else you want to achieve in your life.

- You want to make more money? The secret lies with your health and fitness.
- You want to ignite the passion in your love relationship or attract the partner of your dreams? The path to this paradise starts with your health and fitness.
- You want to be a better role model to your children or cultivate more courage, confidence, and certainty? Yes, you guessed right—it all starts with your health and fitness.

The first step to arriving at your destination is to know what that destination looks like. So what exactly is your vision? What is the outcome you desire? What are the results you want to see? Do you want to get lean, ripped, and shredded with less than 10 percent body fat, or is your goal to always be able to run and play with your grandkids when you're well into your nineties? Do you want to ignite the attraction and desire of your spouse, or do you want to turn heads when you enter a room so that you can attract a partner? There are countless paths to get "there," but first you need to define exactly where "there" is.

"Alice came to a fork in the road. 'Which road do I take?' she asked. 'Where do you want to go?' responded the Cheshire Cat. 'I don't know,' Alice answered. 'Then,' said the Cat, 'it doesn't matter.' "

—*Lewis Carroll,* Alice in Wonderland

Most people start nutrition plans or exercise routines without actually having an end goal in mind. The problem with this is that there is a lot of truth in the cliché: Fuzzy targets don't get hit. So I'm going to share with you exactly how to clarify your target and remove the fuzziness by setting S.M.A.R.T. goals.

S.M.A.R.T. Goals

Setting S.M.A.R.T. goals is not rocket science, and you may have even heard this acronym before, but you would be surprised how many people I've worked with who don't set S.M.A.R.T. goals. As you begin clarifying your vision, make sure that the goals you're setting are S.M.A.R.T. goals. Here's what that means:

S is Specific

Your goals must be clear and specific, which means they can be easily described to another person. You need to know exactly what it is you're attempting to achieve, with no fuzziness at all.

M is Measurable

Your goals must be measurable and quantifiable. You must know when you've achieved them. "I want to lose weight" or "I want to make more money" are not measurable, so they're not good goals. "I want to lose thirty pounds in ninety days" or "I want to make $100,000 by December 31" are measurable goals.

A is Attainable

Make sure your goals are realistic to what you can actually accomplish. If you set the bar too high, you'll know it and you won't get it done. Make sure you've got a good chance of success, so that you can "win."

R is Rewarding

On the other hand, make sure you set the bar HIGH enough that your goal energizes and excites you. You've got to really want it. Start by setting goals small enough to win, but big enough to matter. Once you string together several wins, set much bigger goals that will stretch you beyond your perceived capacity.

T is Time Bounded

A goal without a deadline is a wish. Deadlines make it real and create urgency. Deadlines put pressure on you to get it done. Your goal must have a deadline.

After completing the first step of clarifying your vision, the second step is to set goals that will help you achieve your vision. Then break down these goals into a focused strategic plan with step-by-step daily actions.

Before you define your daily actions though, you must break down your vision into time-bounded goals and supporting benchmarks. Here's what that means: Once you've clarified the vision for where you want to be one year from today, break down that vision into a ninety-day goal. Then take that ninety-day goal and set sixty-day and thirty-day benchmarks to keep you on track toward your ninety-day goal.

Let's say you're a man whose ideal vision is to weigh 175 pounds with 10 percent body fat and your current weight is 225 pounds. So over the next twelve months you will work to drop fifty pounds. Based on this annual goal, you set a ninety-day goal of dropping fifteen pounds. Therefore, you're striving to drop five pounds per month so that your thirty-day benchmark is to weigh 220 pounds and your sixty-day benchmark is to weigh 215 pounds.

After setting your goals and the benchmarks required to achieve your vision, the third step is to define the actions you must take to bring this vision into reality. When it comes to your body, there are two paths that lead you to your results: fitness and nutrition.

Now there are countless actions you could take within each of these paths, but I'm going to share two actions that have worked for me.

1) Sweat every single day.
2) Drink a green smoothie daily.

My first commitment to reach the vision I have for my health and fitness is to be in motion and sweat daily. Yes, you read that right: every single day. This doesn't mean I need to exercise for two hours a day. All I need to do is sweat, which can be done during a workout of just fifteen to twenty minutes.

My second action is to drink a green smoothie every single day. The average person's diet is significantly lacking in fruits and vegetables. So being a busy entrepreneur, I've found that making a green smoothie first thing in the morning is a convenient way to get all of my fruits and vegetables for the day while skyrocketing my energy and fueling my power. So what are your daily actions and habits you're committing to?

The purpose of this exercise is simply to remove the fuzziness from your commitments. When you are crystal clear on your goals and habits, you wake up each morning knowing exactly what actions to take that day to move closer to your vision.

Imagine waking up every single day this week and knowing exactly what your exercise routine will look like. Imagine taking the time to set yourself up for success Sunday night so that your meals are prepared for the week and you no longer fall into the convenience trap of eating whatever is in front of you. What impact would this have on your life? Do you believe this would catapult you into the ideal vision you have for your body?

The fourth and final step is to take massive action. This is where the rubber meets the road. Without your commitment to taking massive action, nothing else you did will matter. Action is what separates people with extraordinary lives from people with mediocre lives.

The Phases of Your Fitness Journey

Now that you have a clearly defined road map, you must understand the three phases that are going to impact your ultimate results.

Phase #1: Mindset

Phase number one is mastering your beliefs. This is the most overlooked phase when it comes to accomplishing your goals in any area of your life, especially regarding your health and fitness. When most entrepreneurs want to get in better shape, they typically think all they have to do is hire a personal trainer and focus on the external things like their exercise and nutrition.

When it comes to reaching health and fitness goals, our exercise accounts for only 20 percent of our results and our nutrition accounts for 80 percent. Our mindset, on the other hand, accounts for 100 percent of our results. Until we master our mindset by overcoming our fears, doubts, and limiting beliefs, our desired results will continue to elude us.

Your beliefs about health and fitness are the foundation of your mindset. And if you don't actually uncover your limiting beliefs, then you will take limited action, yielding limited results. So what exactly are limiting beliefs? A limiting belief is a belief that says: "No matter what I do, I'm going to always be fat because it's in my genes" or "Fitness is just too boring and hard" or "I don't have enough money to invest in the proper nutrition and exercise program" or the most popular limiting belief, "I'm just too busy."

Each of these beliefs is incredibly toxic in your life. If you have limiting beliefs like these, it doesn't matter how clear your vision is, how defined your strategy is, or how committed you are to taking action. You're not going to take the action required to get the results you want.

You have a choice to hold on to your existing limiting beliefs or create new empowering beliefs. Before you start creating your exercise and nutrition plan, you must uncover and clarify what limiting beliefs have held you back.

Most people are unaware of the limiting beliefs they've carried with them their entire life, because their parents, society, and the environments instilled them. By taking the time to uncover your limiting beliefs and reframing them into empowering beliefs, you will gain the certainty and confidence required to take action and achieve the results you want.

Now before I share with you several of my personal

empowering beliefs about health and fitness, I want to briefly explain the subconscious mind's impact on the conscious mind. I learned about this when interviewing TV and radio nutrition and fitness expert Marci Lock.

Imagine for a moment that you were 100 pounds overweight. Really take a moment to think about what that weight would feel like on your body. Try to visualize what you would look like physically. Consider how you would feel mentally and emotionally if you were 100 pounds overweight. Imagine how your self-talk might sound and what your level of energy and confidence would be like. Really close your eyes for a moment and picture yourself being 100 pounds overweight.

Now that you're 100 pounds overweight, imagine telling yourself, "I'm a fat-burning machine" or "I am ripped and have six-pack abs." How likely is it that you would believe yourself? You got it—no chance in hell. It's more likely that you would say to yourself, "Bullshit, I have six-pack abs. I'm 100 pounds overweight and have a long way to go."

The thought of this "empowering belief" is so

unrealistic for someone who is 100 pounds overweight that it is immediately disregarded, proving their old belief systems to be correct that they're overweight, unattractive, and not enough. When people are focusing on shifting their mindset and demolishing limiting beliefs, they must start with a belief that they actually believe to be true. If they choose a belief that is totally unrealistic, then it doesn't matter how many incantations, affirmations, or mantras they do; their subconscious mind will override their conscious mind.

When you create an empowering belief that you can actually believe, you start operating from excited creation energy versus a fear-based energy. So start where you are. If you're 100 pounds overweight, rather than telling yourself, "I am ripped with six-pack abs," tell yourself, "I am happier and healthier every day." Now as long as you're staying committed to the right daily habits, you will believe and begin to feel happier every day.

Here are several of my personal beliefs that have empowered me to take massive action in my health and fitness.

I am in control of my physical destiny.

I have the responsibility for what I put into my body as well as how I use my body. This area of my life is entirely dependent upon self-discipline and self-control. My general daily lifestyle and the small choices I make each day will be the determining factor in how well I live. No one else can do this for me. My health relies solely on me doing what needs to be done.

My body is a machine.

The only real limits my body knows are the ones I set. My physical capabilities stretch as far as I will allow them. My body is a machine that will drive itself into the vision I have for my health and fitness. With each exercise, I strive to push myself just a little bit harder—expand my physical capabilities just a little bit farther. My body heals and regulates on its own with proper input, and performs at an optimal level when it is taken care of. My body is a tool—the vehicle through which I express physical life. As with any tool, I have to know how to properly use it to reap the greatest benefits and take care of it if I want it to last. This means continual knowledge, maintenance, and dedication.

Motion creates emotion.

The single most important factor in being well is using my body. Pushing my limits, growing, and gaining strength, flexibility, and balance are all things that will shake my internal world and get my life flowing. I am highly committed to living in motion and sweating every single day!

My health and fitness is the foundation of my brand.

My body is a temple, a gift I have been given, and my self-discipline in regards to my health and fitness will forever impact my ability to achieve all that I want in life. Tomorrow is the disease that keeps me from reaching my goals. I choose to do it today. My health and fitness affects every single area of my life. It influences my financial abundance, my relationships, my spiritual connection with source, my clarity of thought, my emotions, my energy level, and my certainty and confidence to handle life's adversities.

My life is at stake.

More than any other area of my life, my health determines my quality of life. If I'm not healthy, I'm not stable. If I'm not stable, I compromise my experience with myself and my loved ones. If I don't have my health, I don't have my life.

Feel free to borrow any of these empowering beliefs if they resonate with you or throw them out if they don't. The lesson is that these empowering beliefs lead me to empowered action and yield empowered results.

Phase #2: Motive

Your motive is your purpose. It's the reason you want what you want. This phase is often ignored on the journey to becoming more fit, which is why very few people have the body they want.

There are two different levels of motives that are going to affect your actions. Level number 1 is a shallow motive or purpose. If I ask entrepreneurs why they want to become fearlessly fit and the only reason they give is to look better, then I know there's a high probability they will fail because they only have a surface-level purpose. All of their excuses of not having enough money, enough time, or poor genetics are greater than the shallow motive of just looking better.

The second level that I challenge you to create for yourself is a deep motive or purpose. I'm talking about a burning desire to do what needs to be done so you can get the results you want, no matter what obstacles or challenges stand in your way.

Five years ago, my greatest hero died. My father. I remember that time in my life like it was yesterday. My father had battled alcoholism since he was a teenager and now that he was sixty years old, his life choices led him to cancer and an early death.

Witnessing his quality of life deteriorate in front of my eyes got me thinking about my own existence. I also reflected on how many excuses I had made that allowed me to neglect my own health.

I remember sitting in hospice holding my dying father's hand as he took his last breath, and in that moment, I made the decision to never neglect my health again. In an instant, my shallow purpose of wanting to look better was replaced with a burning desire to make my health the most important aspect of my life.

Sadly, there are many people who reach a point of being so overwhelmed, frustrated, and depressed that they consciously choose to give up on life. I'm now driven by my desire to be a living example of health and vitality and to teach others that they can be healthy and still have massive financial success. I've said it before, but if you're like most entrepreneurs, your primary focus in life is growing your business and making more money. I'll ask you to consider that creating a deeper purpose in your fitness will fuel the success that you want in your business.

Being fit not only gets you paid, but it also provides security to your family. Neglecting your health and fitness, on the other hand, is devastating to both you and your family. So the question is: How bad do you want this? Do you have a shallow motive or do you want to dig deeper and create a more powerful purpose that will push you to take the action necessary to overcome your excuses and obstacles.

Phase #3: Motion

Motion is action—massive action! Taking action will separate you from the millions of struggling entrepreneurs and get you the results you want. Be aware that there are three things that are going to stand in your way or slow down your efforts to take massive action. We've discussed these obstacles various times throughout this book, and I'm sure you've experienced all three: fears, doubts, and limiting beliefs.

Most people think they must get rid of their fears, doubts, and limiting beliefs before they take action. But this misguided belief is actually backwards and keeps people from creating the life of their dreams. The secret to actually overcoming these three obstacles is motion. When you take massive action first, your fears will disappear, your doubts will dissipate, and your limiting beliefs will completely shift into something more empowering.

Now that you understand the 7 fitness lies holding you back, the fearless fitness journey, and the three phases affecting your journey, it's time to shift focus back to your business and specifically your ability to create wealth! In the next chapter, we will dive deep into the mindset required to double, triple, and even increase your income tenfold.

Chapter 4:

Doubling Your Income – *College taught me how to move money around. These entrepreneurs revealed the secrets to creating and growing money... without losing my soul.*

For most of us, money is a subject that tends to be surrounded by mixed signals, mystery, and confusion. We're taught that the love of money is the root of all evil, yet just about everyone we know spends most of their waking hours trying to make more of it. At a young age, I constantly wondered, "What is this thing called money and why is everyone around me so focused on accumulating more of it?"

Money was everywhere I looked, yet nobody talked about it. Not my parents, not my teachers, not my employers, and not my friends. I learned at a very young age that if I wanted to learn about money— what it is, where it comes from, and how it's used—I needed to self-educate myself.

Nobody I knew was going to teach me how to earn it, keep it, and invest it. I was solely responsible for learning all I could on the subject if I wanted to avoid the struggles I witnessed all around me. So as an eighteen-year-old college student, I chose to major in finance hoping to finally learn about this subject.

Despite receiving four years of an invaluable education, I still didn't learn much about money and wealth creation through my college curriculum. I studied accounting, corporate finance, derivatives, micro and macroeconomics. I learned about discounted cash flow models and leveraged buyouts. But none of these classes and lessons directly applied to the subject of making and managing money in my personal life.

So after graduating, I did what every finance student dreams of—I became an investment banker. After more than three years of investment banking, I still didn't understand the subject of money and wealth creation. I knew how to buy and sell companies, but I didn't know how to start my own company or create a product or service that was valuable to the marketplace. At the most basic level, I didn't understand how to create, preserve, and grow my personal financial wealth.

This realization at twenty-five years old led me on my journey to studying money. I began reading books, attending seminars, and hiring mentors/coaches so that I could remove the mystery, chaos, and confusion surrounding money. During the course of my journey, I connected with one of my greatest financial mentors, a man named Jon Butcher. Jon is the founder of a personal development company called Lifebook. Jon is also a serial entrepreneur, having starting over seventeen companies, and is someone who has mastered the subject of money and wealth creation.

Through the Lifebook program, Jon provides the best answer I have ever discovered to the question, "What is money?" Below is an excerpt from Jon's perspective on the subject of money.

The True Nature of Money
By: Jon Butcher, founder of Lifebook

Money is simply a tool of trade. It is a medium of

exchange. Nothing more, nothing less. Money is an invention that allows us to trade the goods we create and the services we offer more easily. It is one of the most important inventions in the history of our species. Without money, civilization would not have been possible.

Money has two primary purposes: to standardize value so that people can trade things more easily, and to store value, so that people can save it to trade at a later date. And these two things are the foundation of the civilized world.

Here is an example of what "standardizing value" means: Say I was a wheat farmer a few thousand years ago, before money was invented. I want some eggs, so I have to barter. I need to find a chicken farmer and try to trade him some wheat for some eggs. But if the chicken farmer doesn't want wheat—if he wants beef instead, now I have to find a man with cows. And if I find the man with cows but he doesn't want my wheat either, say he wants three clay pots instead, now I have to find a potter. Finally! I find the potter and he is willing to trade me three pots for my wheat! Now I can trade the pots for the beef and the beef for the eggs!

That is what people used to have to do to trade their goods and services—trade directly for other people's goods and services. It was really clumsy and inefficient. But money eliminated all of that. As a wheat farmer, the invention of money allowed me to turn my wheat into silver coins. And since everyone in the kingdom recognized those coins as the "standard of value," I could trade them for eggs, beef, pots, and jewelry—anything I wanted in one step. It's infinitely more efficient and allowed civilizations to flourish.

Money is a medium of exchange. It standardizes or equalizes value. It makes everything worth X amount of coins or dollars.

Money also allowed people to store value, which was a remarkable leap forward in the history of commerce. As a wheat farmer, I work all year long in my fields. But the harvest happens all at once. If I don't trade my wheat quickly, it will mold and all my work will go down the drain. So I have to trade my wheat for whatever happens to be available at the time. If I want to trade my wheat for a horse, but there are no horses available at the time, I am simply out of luck. Maybe next year I'll be able to find a horse when I have some more wheat.

Money changed all that too. With money I can turn my wheat into coins and not only trade them for what I want, I can trade them when I want. This makes my wheat so much more valuable, because I can wait a month, six months, or even a year until I find exactly the horse I'm looking for. I can even pass my money onto my children.

Money allowed people to save for the first time in history. And what is it that they were saving? What was contained within that money? Their productive accomplishments. Their ingenuity. Their hard work.

Money is STORED ENERGY. Your work, your sweat, your thinking, your talents are what is contained within the money in your wallet.

Today we use paper money. In America we use dollars. Dollars are pieces of paper printed by the government. By themselves, they are worthless. You can't eat them, you can't live in them, you can't do anything with them other than what it was invented for—to trade products and services. It's not the dollars themselves that have worth—it is only what dollars represent that have worth.

Why is this so important to understand? Because it frees you from chasing those pieces of paper and focuses you instead on the true source of wealth, which is what those pieces of paper represent ...

Money represents the very best things human beings have to offer each other: the goods and services that people produce. With money, people can easily exchange their work, talents and skills—the very best that is inside of them—for the very best that is inside of others. Money is quite literally a symbol of human productivity and achievement. It represents all the good things that we create for each other.

Today, we trade our work for money, which we then use to trade for the work of other people. Steven Spielberg's work is to make movies. And the rest of us go to work, trading our various talents for money; then we trade a small part of what we have earned to Steven Spielberg's company, so we can enjoy an evening's entertainment.

The value Bill Gates has created is software that has changed the way people live. He is wealthy because he has positively affected the lives of literally billions of people in a profound and positive way.

A doctor, a teacher, a lawyer, a janitor all provide valuable services to other people. They exchange those valuable services for money, so they can acquire the valuable services of others. The better they are at what they do, the more valuable they become to others. And the more valuable they become, the more money they will be able to trade their work for. Money is nothing more than a symbol of the best that people have to offer each other.

Do I love money? If you mean do I love little green pieces of paper with pictures of dead presidents on them, the answer is "No, not really." But if you mean do I love what money represents, what it means and what it can do—the answer is "absolutely."

Anyone who has "collecting dollars" at the center of their life's aspirations is missing the point. If you want to enrich yourself, stop concentrating on those little pieces of paper and start concentrating on the value that you can contribute to the people around you, because THAT is the true basis of money. And it's the only true way to create wealth.

Forging a Fearless Financial Mindset

Now that you have a clear understanding of the subject of money, how do you go about doubling or multiplying your income even more? In this section, I'll present actionable strategies to help you accelerate the growth of your wealth, but first it's important to discuss how to create a Fearless Financial Mindset.

In preparing to write this chapter, I interviewed Garrett Gunderson, a *New York Times* best-selling author and world-renowned thought leader on the subject of money and wealth creation.. Garrett has dedicated his career to debunking the many myths and fabrications about money that undermine the prosperity and joy of millions of hard-working, honest business owners. Garrett's company, Freedom FastTrack, empowers its members to build sustainable wealth through financial efficiency and organization, leading to clarity, peace of mind, and financial confidence.

During our interview, Garrett said, "The biggest deterrent from financial freedom is not the economy. It's not the location that you live or the people that you spend most of your time with … No amount of luck, saving, discipline, rate of return, or financial system will matter if you can't conquer the scarcity mentality. The scarcity mindset is the largest destroyer of wealth and the only true solution is by creating an abundant financial mindset."

I completely agree with Garrett that our mindset is critical to creating wealth, especially as I reflect on the scarcity mindset that nearly defeated me when I launched my company. Building a business from scratch with zero cash flow coming in, I endured many sleepless nights being consumed by my fear of financial poverty. I would show up on sales calls needy and desperate, repelling anyone who considered hiring me. It wasn't until I shifted from my scarcity mindset to an abundant financial mindset that my business started to grow.

Abundance is the non-negotiable foundation to a Fearless Financial Mindset. Now you may be thinking, "Yeah, Peter, that sounds great. But I literally have no money. I am struggling financially and have no idea how to create an abundant financial mindset."

If you want more money, you must go to the very core

of what you could do to provide value to this world. Making money isn't about how many resources you have; it's about how resourceful you can be. It's not about having money first; it's about having a deep commitment to being resourceful by creating massive value in the marketplace.

So it begins with your mental capital. What is your knowledge? What is your unique offering? What is your wisdom? What are your tools and systems and the ways that you can serve others? When you translate your mental capital into serving others and solving their problems, you begin building relationship capital.

There are two primary reasons that an entrepreneur may be consumed by financial scarcity. First, they're not reaching enough people to deliver value in exchange for money. Second, they don't have enough value to create and they need to invest in themselves and learn the skill sets that create massive value for their clients.

Garrett's advice for breaking free of the scarcity mindset involves taking immediate action. He suggests calling up people you know—people you can create value for in this world—and instead of telling them your sob story about your poor cash flow or the circumstance you're in, you ask them questions to figure out how you can help them.

So Garrett would call up a friend and say, "What are you excited about in your life right now? What are you working on that's difficult? Where do you want to be that you haven't quite got to yet? What resources do you need to help you reach the next level? Where do you see yourself one year from today?" Garrett advises asking valuable questions until you come across something you can do to provide value.

When we are feeling scarce and we help someone out, that person appreciates and acknowledges us, which puts us in a better mindset. And once we're in a better frame of mind, we can start to see opportunity and stop sulking in the problems in the world or the situations that feel so devastating and defeating. In short, rather than complaining or withdrawing, we must reach out to help others when we're in need.

This one strategy of focusing on serving others when you're in need will open up a new level of production and prosperity that will magnetically shift your scarcity mindset to a financially abundant mindset.

The True Meaning of Financial Freedom

Money is most important to us when we feel like we don't have enough. In a way, it's like oxygen— we don't think about it very much until we don't have it, and then we can't think about anything else. How many times a day do you have thoughts about money that affect your life in a negative way? How often do negative thoughts about money cause you to say, "You know I'd really like to, but …"?

"I'd really like to take that vacation, but …"

"I'd really like to live in that house, but …"

"I'd really like to fly my family to Europe, but …"

"I'd really like to volunteer more, but …"

When we're attached to the idea that we must accumulate a set amount of money before we can take action on our dreams, we're postponing what we want to do today in hopes of "someday" having the money and time to actualize that dream. Now I'm not suggesting you go out and take on considerable debt to fulfill all of your desired experiences and acquire all of your desired possessions. Rather, I'm suggesting that you consider what your life would look like if you shifted your mindset by giving yourself permission to not only have these desires, but to take action toward making those desires a reality.

Where in your life have you no longer allowed yourself to want something, because a "but" immediately shows up on the other side of that desire (i.e., "I'd really like to, but …)?

The shortcut and fastest path to allowing things you desire into your life is through appreciation. Consider approaching money and wealth creation from a place of appreciation rather than a place of neediness or desperation. One of the greatest lessons I learned from my mentor Jesse Elder is that wealth is not a number. Wealth is a feeling. In other words, we don't want that designer outfit, sports car, or enormous mansion. What we want is the feelings that we think those material possessions will give us— feelings of significance, power, respect, and love.

By consciously changing your feeling around wealth,

you will begin to develop a sense of peace and tranquility when thinking about money. And this heightened sense of ease and peace will open you up to greater sums of wealth than you ever imagined.

The money flowing into your life right now is in direct proportion to your comfort level with money. Picture a pipe with water running through it. The more the pipe expands, the more water flows through the pipe. The same is true with your comfort level with money. The more expansive your comfort level with money becomes, the more money will flow into your life.

I once coached a business consultant who desired to raise his rates. His consulting had led to significant results for his clients and he was getting more referrals than ever. At his current rate, he reached capacity in the amount of clients he could take on. Recognizing that he felt he was spreading himself too thin, I challenged him to double his rates.

At first he pushed back in an attempt to stay within his financial comfort zone. As his coach, I knew my job wasn't to make him comfortable. Rather, my job was to challenge him to break through his self-imposed limitations to grow beyond his comfort zone. So during one of our sessions I had him consider the possibility of doubling his rates. His first response was that he would get fewer clients. I said, "Okay, let's assume you do bring in fewer clients at these higher rates. In fact, let's say that you have half as many clients, but with your rates doubled, you get paid the same amount."

I remember seeing him light up at this realization and new possibility. He accepted the challenge of doubling his rates and made the commitment to offer his new pricing that week. During our next session, he reported back that he couldn't find the courage or confidence to make offers at his doubled rates. It was clear to me that his comfort level with money was limiting his ability to charge higher rates.

At this point, I advised him to go to his bank and withdraw an amount of money that he felt nervous carrying on him. The amount we arrived at was $10,000. Twice a day for the next week, I had him pull out and count that bundle of money in the privacy of his home. After doing this for a week, something miraculous happened. He noticed he was feeling less nervous carrying that amount of cash on him. He was no longer living in fear of losing that money. Once he expanded his comfort level with money, he was able to get two new clients at his increased rate.

Does having a large amount of cash on you cause fear? Imagine walking into your bank right now and withdrawing a sizable amount of money. Whether that's $1,000, $10,000, or $100,000, I want you to imagine a sum large enough that you would feel afraid to carry that much money on you. Now why exactly are you afraid of carrying that much cash on you? For most of us, we're afraid because we fear losing it.

Jesse Elder explained in our interview that there are only two limiting beliefs that cause the fear of loss. The first is thinking that the resource was scarce or rare in the first place. I've seen countless entrepreneurs limiting themselves in business because they viewed money as a scarce resource. No matter how much value they created for their clients, they never made enough money because they thought there wasn't enough to go around. The second cause of this fear is believing you don't have the ability to attract or create wealth in the first place.

I'll share a metaphor here to illustrate this reality. Imagine cupping your hands in an effort to transport water. After realizing that the water is trickling out, you decide to squeeze your hands as tight as you can in an effort to hold more water. What happens? That's right, you end up capturing less and less water. The tighter you squeeze water, the less you have.

Whether it's money, love, or happiness, to squeeze tightly is to drive out whatever it is you want to experience. And the fastest way to lose anything is to live in fear of its loss. Conversely, the fastest way to create a fearless financial mindset is to first appreciate the money that is already flowing into your life. Then in a state of active appreciation, focus on closing the gap between the money you're currently making and the money you want to make.

All of the money you want already exists. The problem is that it's in the wrong account. The reason that the money is in the other account is because you haven't done anything worthy to transfer that money into your account. So from this state of appreciating what you already have, clarify the value you can create in exchange for the amount of money you desire.

Fearless Finance Principles
Now that you've got a powerful financial mindset, it's

time to get into actionable wealth creation principles that will immediately transform your financial life.

Fearless Finance Principle #1: Wealth creation is a process, NOT an event.

When I started my coaching business, I remember thinking that all I needed was one big product launch or high-paying client to launch me on the path to financial freedom. I spent my first few months seeking this elusive financial windfall that would create sustainable riches in my business.

Then one day I attended a seminar in San Diego and had the opportunity to listen to Reid Tracy, president and CEO of Hay House Publishing. As I'm listening to the CEO of the largest and most influential self-empowerment publishing company in the world, he shares the story of Wayne Dyer, world-renowned author of over forty books, including twenty New York Times bestsellers. Reid describes how Wayne started out driving from town to town, selling his first book from the trunk of his car. He then turns to the audience and shares a concept that will forever change the way I view wealth creation: "It takes ten years to become an overnight success."

You see, at the time, I was looking at the highly successful authors, speakers, and coaches in my industry and assumed they had always been playing at that level of success. The reality was that they went through years of pain, struggle, and failure before really making it.

From that moment forward, I started viewing wealth creation as a process, not an event. Letting go of my attachment to this elusive event allowed me to focus my time and energy on building the systems and processes that create sustainable and predictable wealth in my business.

MJ Demarco explains in his book The Millionaire Fastlane, "All highly successful entrepreneurs create their wealth from a carefully orchestrated process. Despite what you have heard or read, wealth is not an event. Wealth eludes most people because they are preoccupied with events while disregarding process. Without process, there is no event." Processes are developed behind the scenes over months and years. The events that you see and hear about wouldn't be possible without the process. The event is actually the result of the process.

When the twenty-five-year-old sells his Internet company for $50 million, you read about it on the tech blog. The event is positioned for all to admire. What you don't hear about is the long hours of coding the founder had to endure sitting at a computer. You don't hear about his family discouraging him out of fear that he would fail and lose everything. You don't hear about the tens of thousands of dollars of credit card debt he had to take on to launch his company.

All events of wealth are preceded by process, a behind-the-scenes story of trials and tribulations, of sleepless nights and countless sacrifices. If you try to skip the process, you'll never experience the event.

Fearless Finance Principle #2: Multiple streams of income distract you from a gushing income river.

We're surrounded today by false promises of multiple passive streams of income. So let me bust a bubble myth for you right now. There is nothing passive about creating streams of income. In the beginning, and throughout your business growth process, you must invest a significant amount of time, energy, and money into building your business.

One of the fastest paths to financial ruin is trying to create multiple streams of income before you have one predictable and sustainable source of income.

According to Garrett Gunderson, "Not enough people create focus and depth because they get scattered. We read something about multiple streams of income so we try to create too many streams of income before creating a river. Streams are fine, but I'd rather take the Amazon River that is gushing 4,000 miles of fresh water into the ocean and breathing fresh life all around it. People just don't create that depth because they get overwhelmed from over committing."

So if you have yet to build a predictable and sustainable gushing income river, the next fearless finance principle will change your business and life forever.

Fearless Finance Principle #3: Adhere to the doorman principle.

Jon Butcher and Rick Sapio, two of my mentors, introduced me to "the doorman principle," a concept that has created more focus and depth in my life while minimizing scatter and distraction.

Here's the essence of this principle: Imagine having a "doorman" standing on guard at the "front door" of your life. The doorman's job is to make sure that nothing and no one gets into your life that doesn't belong there.

You must consult your "doorman" every time you meet new people, assess a new opportunity, make a big decision, deal with a big challenge, etc., and ask yourself, "Is this person, is this project, is this 'X' right for me? Should I let this into my life or not?"

The key to this concept is to develop a world-class doorman by defaulting to "no." Most people default to "yes." They say "yes" to every request and every new person who comes into their life. This leads them to feel burned out and overwhelmed. Going forward, make a commitment that you will not allow anyone or anything into your life that doesn't add huge value or propel you toward your vision; practice defaulting to "no."

One of my favorite quotes of all time is by Warren Buffet—and it perfectly illustrates why the doorman principle is so important. He said, "The difference between successful people and highly successful people is that highly successful people say 'no' to almost everything."

Saying "no" to almost everything allows you to say "yes" to the right things. It unlocks time and energy for you to focus on building that gushing income river rather than building trickling streams of income that produce barely enough money to survive.

Fearless Finance Principle #4: Use the net worth accelerator.

The fourth fearless finance principle is the "net worth accelerator," and it states that your net worth increases in proportion to your increases in confidence and self-worth. This brings us back to an earlier topic, because the fastest way to increase your confidence and self-worth is through daily fitness.

Below is an excerpt from an interview I did with Sean Stephenson about how fitness has impacted his ability to make money:

Interview Excerpt with Sean Stephenson

Peter: You are now one of the top paid speakers in your industry. So, how has your commitment to fitness contributed to the growth of your business?

Sean: Well, simply put, you make more money when you feel good. You make more money when you are positive. You make more money when you feel alive. You make more money when you feel the blood pulsing through your extremities and you can take deeper breaths of oxygen. And the fastest way I've found to feel better about myself is through exercise.

When you're consistently exercising, you start making offers and closing new business more confidently. When you feel lethargic, cloudy, and drained from not working out, you walk into a meeting with a prospective client with a weaker inner stance, afraid to swing for the fences, because you don't feel like you could hit a home run. You question the fact that you blew off your workout. How are you going to show up confidently in a meeting when you just blew off your workout?

So I think fitness improves your income in a very

elusive way. I think it's going on in the background. Unless you really sit down and look at the direct correlation, it would be easy to blow it off and say: "Well, it's not directly correlated." But I have experienced that there is a direct correlation even though it's harder to measure.

Now, let's take it one step further. Exercising has a direct impact on your subconscious mind. When you're exercising your subconscious mind sees you and thinks: "Wow, he's taking great care of me today." And when your subconscious mind feels you are taking good care of yourself, your self-worth increases. And when you have a higher self-worth, you ask higher fees because you know you're worth what you're charging.

The more self-worth you feel, the better your performance is going to be, and the more money you're going to make.

As Sean said, when you increase your confidence, you make more money. And the best way to be more confident is to have more energy, have more focus, and feel better about yourself through your commitment to fitness. You see, when you are confident, you take massive action. You do not let fear slow you down. When you are confident, you are more charismatic and you attract more customers.

When you are confident, you get more referrals. People who work with you want to recommend your products and services to their friends and family, because they know that by connecting them to you, they are creating value in their loved ones' lives.

When you are more confident, you are more decisive. You no longer doubt yourself. You are very clear on what you want and the path that will bring those results. When you are more confident, you take bigger risks, which yield bigger rewards.

The primary reason that most entrepreneurs struggle to bust through their own limits is their fear of the unknown and their fear of failure. I know this because these were the exact fears that kept me on the sidelines before taking the leap and launching my business.

When you are so confident that those fears don't slow you down, you take the risks necessary to move your business and your life to the next level. When you are confident, you show up more powerfully and you are more persistent. You speak and operate with poise and authority in front of your clients and through your marketing channels.

Simply put, financial scarcity cannot exist when you feel certain of your ability to create wealth. The worst place for an entrepreneur to operate from is the land of scarcity because from this position you present yourself as needy, desperate, and attached to the sale. And if your prospects sense this needy disposition, they will not work with you.

Being Overweight Costs Your Business Money

During my interview with Marci Lock, she shared a story about one of her clients losing out on money because of his weight. He was a very high-level producer and famous coach who worked with thousands of people a year.

He told Marci that it wasn't until he lost 100 pounds that one of his prospects, a man he had spent years pursuing, finally invested in his high-level coaching program. The primary reason this individual didn't invest in his coaching program earlier was because he, the coach, was so overweight. But when he shed 100 pounds, his prospect noticed the positive transformation and signed on as a client.

Think about that for a minute. Even though it's sad to say, the harsh reality is that our weight matters. When somebody looks at you and sees that your body is out of alignment with health and fitness, there's an internal judgment that says, "How can I trust you to take care of me and teach me business when it looks like you can't even take care of yourself? When it looks like you don't even control your own life?"

This is a truth and reality that cannot be ignored. People are naturally judged by their physical appearance. I am not condoning this judgment; rather I'm conveying the truth. So if you are overweight, then you are literally losing out on money because of this judgment. If that doesn't inspire you to take action, I don't know what will.

Now that you've adopted and embraced the fearless financial mindset and learned the strategies required to double, triple, or even increase your income tenfold, the next chapter will help you discover exactly what it takes to become unstoppable.

Chapter 5:

Becoming Unstoppable – *Ten non-negotiable beliefs you must embrace today and the fastest strategies for integrating them into your life.*

In my coaching and consulting business, I have discovered ten foundational beliefs that are core to who successful entrepreneurs are, and those beliefs are the catalyst that launches them to an elite level in their business. In this chapter, I'm not only going to reveal what those ten beliefs are; I'm also going to teach you specific actionable strategies that will empower you to incorporate these beliefs into your own mindset so that you, too, can become unstoppable.

Before you read this chapter, make sure to take the Unstoppable Entrepreneur quiz at www.fearlessmindsetquiz.com to discover if you have what it takes to become an unstoppable entrepreneur. Did you do it yet? Okay, great. Now let's dive right into the ten foundational beliefs that are core to all unstoppable entrepreneurs.

The Ten Beliefs of the Unstoppable Entrepreneur

Unstoppable Belief #1: I believe in making things happen versus letting things happen.

Unstoppable entrepreneurs believe in the law of cause and effect. They know that happiness, abundance, financial prosperity, and fulfillment do not materialize by sitting on the sidelines of life and hoping they will happen someday. These effects are only actualized when you put in the work required to create those results.

The universal law of cause and effect says that your life is a result of your daily choices and actions. Your choices and actions are the cause; your current life is the effect. What you do with the minutes, hours, and days of your life dictates who you are and what kind of life you have.

Thoughts (backed by focused action) become things …

We are all creators of our own reality. What we focus on with emotion and produce through action is what we will attract and manifest in our experience. The law of attraction is always at work. We all manifest something; the question is, are we creating our world consciously or by default? Most of us live with our thoughts on autopilot and create our world by accident. Instead of making things happen, we let things happen.

Now you may be thinking, what is all this airy-fairy new age talk about the law of attraction? Let me make an important distinction here that all unstoppable entrepreneurs believe. The law of attraction only works if your thoughts are backed by focused action.

Unfortunately, movies like The Secret brainwashed millions of people to believe a lie promising results without effort. There's a scene in this movie portraying a man hoping and wishing for checks to show up in the mail. Next thing you know he opens his mail and checks magically appear out of thin air. This is not reality. This is a direct contradiction of the law of cause and effect.

So if you are truly committed to becoming an

unstoppable entrepreneur, you must start by believing in making things happen versus letting things happen.

Action Step: Clarify what you are committed to making happen by reciting a short but empowering affirmation each morning. This can set the tone for your entire day and motivate you on a subconscious level. By reciting your personal affirmation out loud each morning, you take the first step toward committing to your goals. Here are a few affirmations that you can start with:

- Today I will treat my body like the irreplaceable treasure it is. I will eat right, I will exercise, and I will take great care of my physical self. Today I will feel great.
- Today I will practice the character traits I want to build into my life. In particular, I will focus on self-discipline, because that will affect all of the choices I make today.
- Today I will spend twenty minutes connecting with my higher life purpose through meditation.
- Today I will create immense value for the people around me and earn a profit proportionate to that action.
- Today I will advance confidently toward my life

vision. I will end this day in a better, more beautiful place than where I began this morning. I am dedicated to doing this every day of my life.

Unstoppable Belief #2: I prefer risk with the potential of big rewards over security/safety with limited rewards.

Unstoppable entrepreneurs are risk takers. Do you think Richard Branson, Steve Jobs, or Mark Cuban built their empires without taking significant risks? Of course not. The moment you become an entrepreneur and decide to start your own company, you have walked away from the security and safety provided by a steady paycheck.

Does preferring risk mean that entrepreneurs don't feel fear? Of course not. Launching my coaching business the day I lost my sole source of income was one of the scariest experiences of my life. But the rewards I've reaped from taking this risk are rewards that I could never have experienced as an employee.

Of course there are different stages of risk. When you are just launching your business, you are going to have to stomach significant risk, know that you will make lots of mistakes, and be highly flexible and willing to change. After your business has become more established, you'll be more focused on what Tony Robbins calls "asymmetric risk."

Asymmetric risk is taking the least amount of risk that yields the greatest rewards. This is the holy grail of entrepreneurship and investing. But in order to create the capital you need to preserve and grow through asymmetric risk, you must take significant risks at the start of your journey.

If you are risk averse, you simply don't have what it takes to become an unstoppable entrepreneur. Fear of loss, fear of the unknown, and fear of failure will stop you in your tracks.

Action Step: Ask yourself, "What am I willing to risk to achieve my dream?" and capture everything in a list. The clearer you get on the risks you're willing to take and the more comfortable you are with the downside of those risks, the more action oriented you will be. And the more action oriented you are, the greater results you will achieve.

Unstoppable Belief #3: I'm driven by a purpose that is bigger than me or anything around me (it's not just about the money).

As an entrepreneur, you may experience very dark times. It's not easy building a business from scratch and creating something that did not previously exist. There will be breakdowns, challenges, losses, and failures. These are all part of the entrepreneurial journey. At times like these, entrepreneurs who are truly unstoppable are driven by something more than money.

If I knew how difficult being an entrepreneur was when I started out, it's questionable if I would have made the leap. If I knew the sleepless nights and countless sacrifices that would be necessary to actualize my vision, I may have stayed an employee.

I don't say this to scare you or to deter you from taking your business to the next level. I say this to give you a heavy dose of reality so you will really gut check yourself and see if you have what it takes to become an entrepreneur.

For me, it was never just about the money. Sure, I knew that I could make more money as a business owner than I could ever make as an employee. But if it were just about the money, I would have burned everything to the ground long ago. So what drives me to continue to build my coaching company?

It's a purpose that is bigger than me or anything around me. It's a belief that my message will have a significant, positive impact on the world. It's a belief that I was called to go through my painful life experiences in order to learn certain lessons that I could share with others.

There will be days when you don't feel like getting out of bed. There will be days when you don't feel like prospecting for new clients or even fulfilling your commitments to your existing clients. This is all part of the human experience.

The question is, are you driven by a purpose that inspires you to stay committed despite what you may be feeling in the moment? Are you driven by a purpose that propels you to do what you know needs to be done when it needs to be done—whether you feel like it or not? If the answer is "yes," then you are well on your way to becoming an unstoppable entrepreneur.

Action Step: Take fifteen to thirty minutes to think about and write out your purpose for being an entrepreneur. Why are you building the business you are building? Is it to support the lifestyle you want for you and your family? Is it to have a significant impact on the world? Is it to create financial freedom so you never have to worry about money again? Once you've brainstormed your "why's," choose one that inspires you and compels you to take action. Write that on a whiteboard or Post-it note and display it where you will see it often. Perhaps put it near your phone so you can read it when you are struggling with difficult conversations. This purpose will keep you committed when times are tough.

Unstoppable Belief #4: I truly believe I can handle anything life throws at me.

This is a non-negotiable belief that is foundational to becoming an unstoppable entrepreneur. It's a state of being. It's an inner strength that empowers you to handle any adversity that comes your way. Facing adversity and challenge is unavoidable as an entrepreneur. So do you believe you can handle anything life throws at you?

Becoming an unstoppable entrepreneur is not for the weak willed, lazy, or faint of heart. You're simply not going to become unstoppable if you're going to fold in the face of every challenging situation.

There will be people on your journey who are there to drag you down—people who literally want to see you fail. You're going to have to make some tough choices along the way, some of which won't make you very popular. This journey to becoming an unstoppable entrepreneur is going to take courage, perseverance, emotional fortitude, determination, self-discipline, and inner strength. Do you think you have what it takes?

Action Step: If you haven't already, make sure to take the Unstoppable Entrepreneur quiz at www.fearlessmindsetquiz.com to discover if you have what it takes to become an unstoppable entrepreneur.

Unstoppable Belief #5: I am willing to take massive action despite not having a crystal clear vision.

Clarity is a result, not a requirement. Most people

watch their entire lives pass them by, waiting for the clarity they feel is necessary before they take action toward creating the life of their dreams.

As an unstoppable entrepreneur, you will have to leap off the cliff of uncertainty and build your wings on the way down. This is because when you're creating something that did not formerly exist, you will simply not know the best route to developing your creation— at some point, you will simply need to begin by taking action.

I'm not suggesting that taking time to clarify your vision isn't important. It's massively important for you to think through the potential paths you could take. But I'm advising you not to become dependent on achieving that clarity. The moment you take your first step, the more obvious your next step becomes.

Picture yourself in a dark cave with a flashlight. Your light illuminates a portion of the cave, but anything outside the flashlight's beam is pitch black. It's not until you start moving, and take steps toward your destination, that your light begins to illuminate what lies ahead.

Clarity is a result, not a requirement.

Action Step: Detach yourself from needing to know every step of your journey. Do your best to set goals and break those goals down into benchmarks. Then commit yourself to take that first step, even if you're not sure it's the right step. By taking this first step, you are conditioning yourself to take action despite not having a crystal clear vision.

Unstoppable Belief #6: I believe that I am the primary decision maker at the center of my own existence.

This is a belief that I learned from my mentor Jon Butcher, and it's a belief that has shaped my existence. Jon says,

> Your life is yours. You own it. You choose who you spend time with, you choose the books you read and the TV shows you watch, you choose the way you treat people, you choose what to focus on every day …

You are in control of your own existence.

And you can choose to live any way you want to live. You can choose anywhere you want to live. You can choose to do anything you want to do. You can choose to be any kind of a person you want to be. You can shape your life any way you want to shape it.

Imagine operating your life from this belief. Most people live their lives on other people's terms. They go through life needing to please their family, friends, business partners, or society at large. Imagine the freedom that is created when you believe that you are the primary decision maker at the center of your own existence.

One of the most profound ways I've ever heard this belief portrayed was in the documentary *Steve Jobs: The Lost Interview*. Of course, Apple founder Steve Jobs was one of the greatest business executives, product developers, and innovators who has ever lived. Here's how Jobs described this way of life:

When you grow up, you tend to get told that the world is the way it is and your job is just to live your life inside the world. Try not to bash into the walls too much. Try to have a nice family, have fun, save a little money …

That's a very limited life. Life can be much broader once you discover one simple fact: —Everything around you that you call life was made up by people that were no smarter than you. And you can change it, you can influence it, you can build your own things that other people can use.

The minute that you understand that you can poke life and actually something will pop out the other side, you can change it, you can mold it. That's maybe the most important thing. It's to shake off the erroneous notion that life is there and you're gonna live in it versus embrace it, change it, improve it, make your mark upon it.

I think that's very important and however you learn that, once you learn it … you'll never be the same again.

At the end of the day, unstoppable entrepreneurs live life on their terms. They don't seek permission or approval from others. They choose to shape the world to their desired reality. Among these ten unstoppable entrepreneur beliefs, this belief is the most important.

Action Step: Take an honest assessment of your life and remove what you don't want in it by creating a "stop doing list." This week, notice every single thing you do that isn't moving your life forward. Now create a list of the things or activities you're willing to get rid of: an hour of email, TV, or computer time? Are there chores in your life that you can delegate? What about spending time with people who drag you down and drain your energy? Create this list now and commit to sticking to it for the next seven days. Then reassess what you want to keep and what you want to permanently remove from your life.

Unstoppable Belief #7: I believe that money making and creating wealth are very good things.

"Money is one of the most important things in the world. Money represents health, strength, honor, generosity and beauty just as conspicuously and undeniably as the lack of it represents illness, weakness, disgrace, meanness and ugliness."

Money is a symbol of human productivity and achievement. At its essence, money is the by-product of value creation. It is a tool that is earned by creating value in the world around you.

If you lack the belief that money making and creating wealth are very good things, you will never reach your full financial potential. This is because no matter how skilled you become at creating wealth, if you see it as bad or dishonorable, you will do everything in your power to rid yourself of that wealth.

Unstoppable entrepreneurs have the capacity of generating massive wealth because they perceive wealth to be honorable. They perceive money to be a fair exchange for the value their products and services create. When you begin to believe that money making and wealth creation are good things, you will unlock your fullest capacity to double, triple, and even increase your income tenfold.

Action Step: Take a moment to answer the following questions:

- How does money improve your health and

vitality?

- How does money improve your emotional well-being?
- How does money improve your love relationship?
- How does money improve your relationship with your children?
- How does money improve your quality of life (ability to have the experiences and possessions you desire)?

Unstoppable Belief #8: I consistently set goals and commit to habits that empower me to accomplish my goals.

Achieving the vision you have for your ideal life comes down to the goals you set and the daily habits you practice. Aristotle said, "We are what we repeatedly do. Excellence, then, is not an act, but a habit."

As powerful as goals are, they're not enough. You see, goals by their very nature are episodic—they come and go. They are things to be achieved and once you accomplish them, they get crossed off your list.

Habits by their very nature are ongoing. They never

get crossed off the list. They're behaviors and actions that happen consistently and rhythmically over time.

Here's the big secret you've never been told …

Goals are the key to creating great habits and habits are the key to accomplishing your goals. My mentor Jon Butcher taught me that you must consciously set a goal to create a habit to accomplish your goals.

As an entrepreneur, I've created the daily habit of creating and communicating content with my marketplace. Are there days when I don't feel like creating content? Of course. But this habit is the key to generating more leads and converting those leads to clients. Without this commitment, my message would die inside of me.

So if you're committed to becoming an unstoppable entrepreneur, you must consistently set goals and commit to habits that empower you to accomplish those goals.

Action Step: Write out the daily actions and habits you must take to generate more leads and sales in your business. What activities will lead to these two results?

Could it be creating a new sales funnel or marketing campaign? Leads and sales are the lifeblood of your business, so take a moment to clarify the habits that result in more leads and sales.

Unstoppable Belief #9: I am comfortable with having difficult conversations.

To reach an elite level in your business, you must get comfortable with having difficult conversations. If you're going to spin off into an argument with every little bump in the road—every detail that doesn't go your way—you're going to have a lot of trouble reaching that next level in your business.

It takes emotional fortitude to show empathy and listen to another's perspective when what you really want to do is have a self-indulgent emotional outburst. However, if you really want to live your life to the fullest and create the business of your dreams, you've got to show up with some inner strength in challenging conversations.

The fastest path to getting comfortable with having uncomfortable conversations is through honesty, authenticity, and vulnerability. The sooner you speak the truth, the sooner you will liberate the other person to speak his or her truth. The moment the other person understands your agenda, and doesn't feel like you are about to go on the attack, he or she will open up to a deeper conversation.

Achieving this level of comfort doesn't happen overnight. It's like building a muscle. You need to have numerous uncomfortable conversations before you can finally free yourself from the discomfort. Imagine your life where you spoke only the truth. You had nothing to hide and no secrets. How would that level of honesty free you up to create to your fullest capacity?

Action Step: Have a conversation today with someone you've been avoiding. Whether it's with your partner or spouse, a friend, or a client, pick up the phone and do what you've been avoiding.

Unstoppable Belief #10: I'm willing to invest in myself to accelerate the achievement of my goals.

When I launched my business from scratch, I had no idea what the hell I was doing. I didn't know what my message was, who my target client was, or how I could create value in the marketplace. Could I have figured out all of this on my own? Of course. But rather than wasting time and energy spinning my wheels hoping to get some traction, I decided to invest $20,000 in myself by hiring a mentor and joining a mastermind group so that I could accelerate my results. Below is a personal letter I wrote my mentor Garrett J. White after realizing the value of investing in a mastermind group.

My Letter to Garrett J. White, Creator of Wake Up Warrior

Dear Garrett,

Fourteen months ago I was broke, scared, and alone. I had just lost my sole source of income and a love relationship that I thought could last forever abruptly ended. I had no self-worth, felt disconnected from my purpose, and had no idea how to make money to pay my rent.

I was terrified when you told me the investment required to join your mastermind. I didn't have that sort of money at the time, but the voice inside my head said find a way. So I became resourceful ... I borrowed from family and took on debt to make this investment in myself.

The results in my life over the last fourteen months are nothing short of miraculous:

- I launched a coaching business from scratch and am now coaching ten clients who are paying me more than I ever imagined.
- I moved from sleeping on a half-inflated air mattress on the floor of an empty apartment to a beautiful condo overlooking the Pacific Ocean in San Diego.
- I went from feeling no self-worth to creating a deep, satisfied sense of self and self-knowing.
- I learned to live my purpose in life every day and created a business to support the lifestyle I desire.
- I gained deeply authentic and meaningful friendships.
- I became a published author

Above and beyond these results, there are three lessons I learned through you that will forever change my life:

Lesson #1: My Darkness Is My Greatest Gift

I ignored the darkness of my past for the majority of my life. I blocked out the pain of my parents' alcoholism and drug addictions … until you guided me to see the light in my darkness … to see that my greatest life lessons have come from my most painful experiences … to see that there is a message hidden deep inside the "mess" of my life. You helped me uncover this truth and therefore have liberated me to share my message with the world and transform lives as a result.

Lesson #2: Be Real, Raw, and Relevant

The truth is the only thing that will set me free. I learned to stop lying about my needs, wants and desires. I learned that raw honesty is the only path to paradise and that the world conspires for your greatness when you choose to show up real and raw. I learned to stop lying to myself and others about reality.

Lesson #3: Do the Work

As Christopher Stubbs once said, "You don't get what you want. You don't get what you think you deserve.

You get what you're *committed* to!" The reason I got the results above is because I became highly committed to doing the work. There was no way to avoid the work and get the results I desired. So I took massive action despite my fears, doubts, and limiting beliefs. I launched my podcast, started posting raw videos to Facebook, and shamelessly shared my message with the world.

Brother, I just want you to know how much I love you. You guided me over the last fourteen months on my rite of passage from boyhood to manhood, and for that I am forever grateful.

Live Your Life Fearlessly,

Peter Scott IV

As I said before, hiring a mentor and joining a mastermind group is one of the best investments you can ever make. Having somebody in your corner who already has the results you desire will only accelerate your achievement of those results. And to do it within a group of like-minded people who are experiencing similar challenges and striving toward similar goals creates breakthroughs that would not be possible on your own.

If this is something you're searching for, then I encourage you to go to http://thefearlesslifeacademy.com and apply for one of our upcoming events.

It doesn't matter where you are in business. I hired my first mentor the same week I lost my sole source of income. It doesn't matter how many resources you have, what matters is how resourceful you are.

Can you achieve results on your own? Absolutely. But why not shorten the learning curve by investing in someone who already has created the results you desire?

Action Step: Find a mentor who has already created the results you desire. Reach out to potential mentors to see if they are willing and able to support you in achieving these results. If you can't afford to hire these mentors, consider their more affordable programs and products so that you can still learn from them. There is no faster path I'm aware of to becoming an unstoppable entrepreneur than investing in yourself.

Strategies for Becoming Unstoppable

Let's face it, there are going to be days when you aren't feeling unstoppable. I experience these days just like everyone else. So what should you do when this happens? Below are three strategies that have helped me get back into my power when feeling powerless:

Ask Quality Questions

I learned about this strategy when interviewing my friend, TV and radio nutrition and fitness expert Marci Lock. During this interview Marci shared that 98 percent of people stop pursuing a dream or goal after two or three attempts. In other words, they fail one or two times and completely give up. This habitual routine of giving up the moment something becomes challenging limits one's capacity to become unstoppable.

The moment they experience resistance, fear of failure begins to fill their mind. Fear of disapproval and judgment from others overrides their commitment to taking action. Rather than asking themselves quality questions about how they could take a new approach, they accept their judgmental answers such as, "I'm not good enough, smart enough, talented enough, or attractive enough."

By asking yourself quality questions, you can retrain your mind so that you're no longer fixed on right, wrong, good, or bad judgments. And the most toxic judgment is how we judge ourselves in relation to others.

Theodore Roosevelt once said, "Comparison is the thief of all joy." The moment you compare yourself to me or somebody else, you shut yourself down and start judging what's right and what's wrong. When you are comparing yourself to others, it is impossible to be unstoppable.

So rather than dwelling on why things aren't the way you want them to be, focus on asking quality questions by accepting the truth of your current reality and harnessing the curiosity of what it would take to create a new reality. The quality of questions that you ask determines the quality of life you're going to live.

Minimize Negative Self-Talk

Committing to a daily ritual and rhythm that includes exercise minimizes negative self-talk, which is crucial to becoming unstoppable.

When most people neglect their health and fitness, they have an inner dialogue that is constantly negative. Imagine what happens when you're faced with a challenge, and your mind is telling you how worthless you are. Do you think you will have the courage and confidence to take that challenge head-on? Or will you tuck your tail and retreat from the challenge?

This harmful inner dialogue makes it impossible to become unstoppable. However, when you free up the space in your mind that was once occupied by negative self-talk, you are able to focus more on your business and other important areas of your life. For example, you're able to focus on and be more present with your family when you feel good about yourself.

On the other hand, when you're distracted and not present with your family, your power begins to erode because you feel guilty for not connecting with your loved ones. How do you think this affects your ability to be productive in your business? Minimizing negative self-talk is a foundational strategy to becoming unstoppable.

Convert Fear into Fuel

According to serial entrepreneur and founder of the Next Level Experience (www.thenextlevelexperience.com), Raul Villacis, "What you do the first hour after you wake up determines the rest of your day."

Raul teaches processes that he has learned from some of the most successful people in the world, including Tony Robbins, Richard Branson, Steve Forbes, and many others. His exclusive formula known as The Ritual, which creates a daily re-conditioning in the subconscious mind, has brought him success and fulfillment in everything he does.

I had the privilege of interviewing Raul for this book and asked him to share the best practices from The Ritual so that you could implement them in your own life.

There are four phases to The Ritual.

Phase number one is gratitude. Raul suggests taking

just three to five minutes of your time to state or write down the things you already have that you're grateful for. He said, "If you just do this one thing (cultivate daily gratitude), your life will transform before your eyes."

Most people focus on what they don't have versus being grateful for what they do have. Thinking, "I don't have enough money" or "I don't have enough time" creates a scarcity mindset that limits people's ability to take action to achieve the results they want.

Once you find that gratitude, it's time to move onto the second phase of The Ritual, which focuses on kicking up your energy. This is an important phase because without energy, it doesn't matter how grateful you feel; you must have the energy to take the action necessary to get the results you want.

Fortunately, you can create energy at any moment of your life through moving your body. So to wake the body up during The Ritual, Raul combines exercise (such as pushups, running, burpees, or air squats) with listening to empowering music to get into that state of high energy.

This music acts as an anchor that continues to elevate his energy. During this process, Raul also starts to recite empowering affirmations such as, "I have all the time that I need" and "Money is an exchange of value and I produce more value than anyone else." Through this process, Raul will recite thirty to forty affirmations that he knows to be true, thereby conditioning his subconscious mind to start believing these affirmations.

Phase three of the The Ritual is visualization. The key with this phase is to visualize exactly what you want to experience while you're filled with gratitude and energy. This visualization process makes you feel certain that you will accomplish what you are envisioning.

Do you have an important sales call to make? Envision it. Do you have a crucial presentation to make at a board meeting? Envision it. Do you have a challenging conversation with your spouse or children coming up? Envision the outcome you want.

The visualization phase cannot be ignored, because this process allows you to focus on the things that matter most to you. When you have a crystal clear vision, and know exactly what you want, it becomes simple to stay focused on the most important action steps to bring that vision into reality. Without a clear vision, you cannot make the distinction between an opportunity and a distraction. So this visualization allows you to be more decisive and only say "yes" to the opportunities that are going to move you toward your vision.

Phase four of the The Ritual is embracing your fears. While envisioning your deepest fears coming true, listen to a powerful song that anchors your fear so you can experience what you imagine would be the worst-case scenario. You might envision losing that top client, losing all your money, or losing your family. Anchor these fears through music so that you deeply feel what these experiences would be like. Once you embrace these fears, you can release them because you realize through this visualization that they are simply an illusion created by your mind.

Fear is nothing but an illusion of the things you think "could" happen. So rather than ignoring your fears, Raul suggests you anchor and fully experience those fears and then release them. Feeling your worst scenario in your mind and body gives you the confidence and certainty to handle it in the real world. And by embracing and visualizing your deepest fears at the beginning of each day, you will become unstoppable for the remainder of the day since you've already handled in your mind your biggest challenges. This allows you to leverage your darkness and turn your fears into fuel.

Create Space in Your Mind Through Meditation

Your capacity to make money skyrockets when you meditate. Now I realize that's a bold statement, so hear me out. I struggled to commit to a meditation practice for years because I thought I was "too busy" to meditate. I found when I sat down to start meditating, I would dwell on the million other things that needed to be done. I was a victim of my thoughts.

Today, meditation has become a non-negotiable in my life. It's a practice that enables me to be in control of my experiences. Rather than emotionally reacting to something that triggers me, I consciously respond with purpose. Through meditation, I discovered the ability to control my emotions and thoughts. It has allowed me to create space between my response and the event that triggered me.

Nothing has changed outside of me, but my inner state has slowed way down. Athletes call this "flow." The greatest benefit I've received from meditation is certainty. This elevated level of certainty has made me more decisive and, as a result, I am making more money and feeling unstoppable.

If you want to be more present and feel more grounded, I recommend committing to a practice of regular meditation. Now the question is, how do you meditate? Although there are countless meditation techniques, I'll share the one I use.

I carve out twenty minutes every morning to be silent and still through meditation. While sitting in a comfortable position, I close my eyes and focus on the inhaling and exhaling of my breath, sometimes counting the seconds. Inhale—1, 2, 3, 4. Exhale—1, 2, 3, 4. Oftentimes I will silently recite mantras in my mind. Before I share my mantras with you, let me explain a few key things about how mantras work.

A mantra is a sound or idea that you use as a focal point in meditation. In some meditation systems, the mantra is a word or sound from an ancient language, such as Sanskrit or Hebrew. In other systems it might be an idea, such as, "Focus your awareness on your breathing."

You focus your attention on the mantra. Then, when your attention wanders, you go back to the mantra. The mantra gives you a home base to return to whenever you notice that your mind has taken an excursion into the past or the future. The mantra is designed to help you return to the present moment.

For example, if you're using "Om" as your mantra, you repeat "Om" lightly in your mind. After some repetitions, your mind will naturally wander. When you notice that it's wandered, you let go of the thoughts and return to repeating "Om." In Buddhist practices, such as Vipassana meditation, breath awareness is often used as the mantra. You focus your awareness on the sensations of your breathing; then, when you notice that your attention has wandered off into other thoughts, you gently return your awareness to your breathing.

The art of meditation is in the way you let go of your wander-thoughts and return to the mantra. Specifically, it's the art of letting go of the wander-thoughts and returning to the mantra without giving yourself a hard time about wandering.

It's common in the beginning stages of meditation to criticize yourself when your mind wanders, to think of meditation as a conflict between your mantra and your wander-thoughts. As your practice matures, though, you usually realize that criticizing yourself for your mind's wandering is just another thought. You let go of it and return to the mantra. Gradually the habit of self-criticism disappears and is replaced by an openhearted feeling of self-acceptance.

Brian Johnson, the founder of "PhilosophersNotes," recommends approaching meditation like brushing your teeth. It's not supposed to be something you get frustrated with if you do it wrong. In fact, there is no wrong way to do it. You just make the commitment to meditate every single day, and over time, you begin to master your mind and control your thoughts.

Below are several of my mantras that focus my mind and put me in a powerful state:

- "I am the source of my own happiness and fulfillment."

- "I unconditionally love and accept myself."
- "I am the source of my own validation and approval."
- "I create immense value and earn a profit proportionate to that action."

Every time I finish a meditation session I feel more present, certain, and unstoppable. When starting out, I recommend you commit to only five minutes of meditation daily. The key is consistency, not the length of time. Once you're comfortable at five minutes, increase it to ten minutes. Continue increasing your time until you reach a daily meditation practice of twenty minutes.

Now that you've discovered the foundational beliefs and strategies of unstoppable entrepreneurs, it's time for you to take control of your environment and demolish distractions so that you can operate at your peak performance.

Chapter 6:

Excelling in Your Environment – *How to create a work environment that stimulates and inspires your greatness.*

Entrepreneurs have the freedom to consciously create their environment and set themselves up for success. I remember not having such freedom during my investment banking days. I would spend eighty-plus hours per week practically chained to my cubicle crunching numbers under dull florescent lights. Sure, the corner offices for the firm's managing directors were gorgeous, but the cubicle pit for all the financial analysts was not conducive to optimal performance.

I share this with you to remind you of the incredible freedom you have to create your own environment. For those of you reading this who are in less control of your environment, à la my investment banking days, my intention is for this chapter to illuminate actionable strategies that you can still implement to set yourself up for success.

Why are we so affected by environment? Have you ever been in a really great mood and then met up with a friend who was feeling down? What happened to your mood? Odds are your energy level dropped instantly. Often we feel we need to match our energy and intensity with our friends' level—even though moments before they showed up, we were feeling on top of the world.

The same thing happens with our work environment. If you're in a space that is calm, relaxed, and inspiring, you are naturally going to mirror—to some degree—that environment. Conversely, if you are in an environment where you are constantly interrupted by phone calls, emails, and instant messages, the space is dead and dreary, and the lighting is awful, you're going to be lacking in energy, focus, and clarity. It is nearly impossible to get work done in an environment like that. So, knowing that our environment can affect us negatively or positively, it's important to consciously create a space that makes us highly productive. Let's look at how to do this.

Identify Your Ideal Workspace

Identifying and creating your ideal work environment is one of the most overlooked productivity tactics. Right now, I'm writing this book from a cabin in the mountains, secluded from the demands and distractions of my everyday life. I have no access to email, social media, texting, or phone calls. I consciously scheduled six days of pure isolation so that I could focus solely on writing this book.

Giving myself permission to temporarily unplug from my obligations and disconnect from the demands on my time has created space for me to make more progress on my book in six days than I would have in a month back home. Aside from the occasional hike, run, or meditation to break up my day, the only thing I'm focused on is writing. Environment matters.

But how did I figure out that this space was so conducive to creating? Well, that takes some reflection.

Where have you been in the past when you've done your best work? What was the space like? Was there music? Was it bright or dark? Was it loud or quiet? Everyone has a different ideal space. Identify yours.

Identify Your Ideal Work Time

Next, it's important to identify the time of day when you are most productive. Some people are morning people and some people are night owls. Which one are you? Although many people will disagree, I don't believe there's a one-size-fits-all approach to identifying the time of day when you are most productive.

Sean Stephenson, author of *Get Off Your "But,"* is a night owl. His optimal work time is from 9 p.m. to 1 a.m., after he has had dinner and spent some time with his wife. I, on the other hand, find my most creative juices flowing early in the morning. I feel most creative and typically do my most productive work from 6 to 10 a.m. What time of the day do you feel most engaged and focused?

Note: If you have a 9-5 job, then pick a time that is closest to your optimal time of day for productivity. There is no shortage of hours in the day, only a shortage of commitment.

Identify Your Challenges

Just as important as discovering what space and time produces your best efforts, it's equally important to identify which environments keep you from doing your best work. So ask yourself: Where is it most challenging for me to work? What is the environment like? (Light, dark, loud, bland, etc.) Why is it so challenging for me to work there? (Constant chatter, phones ringing, no inspiration, etc.)

Once you've identified these anti-productive environments, acknowledge them and avoid them like a bad ex. Nothing good will come from them.

Consider Listening to Music

Some people work extremely well when they have music in the background. Others don't. If music helps get you focused, then by all means use this natural stimulator. Personally, I love music and play it in the background to help me shift into a state of increased productivity when I'm working on certain projects.

Generally speaking, I've found that music with lyrics is much more distracting than instrumental music.

Listening to soothing music that plays at sixty beats per minute can decrease neural activity and lead to a relaxed, but awake, state called alpha state, which is defined by an increase in alpha brain waves and a decrease in higher activity beta waves. Increases in alpha waves have been tied to a psychological state of decreased self-awareness, timelessness, and motivation known as "flow." This flow state is what you want your music to help you reach. If you find the type of music you're listening to is distracting you, then search for another type that gets you into flow.

One of the best resources I've found that leverages this sixty-beat-per-minute music to get into flow is called Focus@Will. Focus@Will is a neuroscience-based audio service that offers specially sequenced instrumental music designed to increase your attention span up to 400 percent when working and studying while helping you effortlessly zone out distraction. If this resource sounds valuable to you then check it out at www.focusatwill.com.

Create Your Productivity Sanctuary

Now that you've identified where you have worked best in the past, the time of day you feel most engaged and focused, the challenging spaces to avoid, and the music that inspires you, it's time to put it all together.

Choose a time of day and a space that works best for you—or if the space isn't always accessible (like this cabin in the middle of the mountains)— then go about creating one that is.

For me, I work best when I'm listening to instrumental music in an environment that is calm and free of distractions. As a result, I like to work between 6 and 10 a.m., early afternoons, and early evenings. I also prefer plenty of sunlight and nature so I spend most of my work hours on my balcony overlooking the Pacific Ocean.

Put these elements together and create a space that meets your unique needs and fuels your productivity.

Action Steps:

1) Write down where you have been in the past when you've done your best work.
2) Identify the time of day you feel most engaged and focused.
3) Write down in detail the environments that have been most challenging for you to work in.
4) Consider whether music puts you in the productivity zone. If so, identify what specific songs or artists and with what business activities.
5) Put it all together to create a space that supports you.

Now that you've crafted your perfect productivity environment, it's time to eliminate distractions and get to work.

Chapter 7:

Demolishing Your Distractions – The subtle shifts for eliminating distractions and getting the right things done so you can create the life you actually want to live.

Distractions are one of the greatest limitations to our productivity. They threaten us all. Whether it's family interruptions, Facebook, the phone, or that in-box that grows like a weed, distractions are very real and we have to deal with them.

One of the biggest reasons we get distracted is because we haven't adequately managed our time. We work when we feel like it or with no end in sight. As an entrepreneur, you always have things to work on, which makes it even more important to control your time. Let's look at how to do it effectively.

Reclaim Control of Your Day

Guarding your work time is part art and part science. If you follow these five steps, you'll be well on your way to taking back control of your day.

Step #1: Set up a schedule with an end time.

Some people are averse to schedules, while others thrive on them. For most of us, schedules give structure to our day. This is something that often goes out the window when you run your own company.

I personally struggled with this when I launched my coaching business. Coming from the corporate world as an investment banker, I was used to a very structured work schedule. So I decided to implement a similar schedule at home. I approached my day the same way I approached my corporate workdays, blocking out chunks of time to focus on one task or another, trying to advance a project toward a specific goal.

How does this apply to you? If you struggle with distractions, set up a work schedule for yourself and …

Step #2: Make it a habit.

We've talked a lot throughout this book about the importance of habits. By now you know that if this schedule is something you stick to only sporadically, you will never reach your full potential. So, once you've established a schedule for yourself, the next and most important step is to actually stay committed to it.

You must protect your workspace just as you should protect your time away from work. Both are equally important and compromising on either one won't help you achieve your goal.

Step #3: Turn off the distractions and close the door.

Today, we are more distracted with technology than we have ever been in history. Hearing our phone ring or vibrate every couple minutes from social media updates, emails, text messages, or phone calls diverts our attention from the task at hand. In an effort to turn off the never-ending distractions, I put my phone on "airplane mode" for blocks of focus time throughout the day. These are one- to two-hour blocks of time where I completely eliminate the distractions so that I can focus on the task before me.

When I worked in investment banking, the managing directors had offices with a door. As an entrepreneur, you must exercise your right to close your door, whether that's literal or not. An open-door policy means you are open to distractions. When you're creating, close the door and give yourself the space you need. Turn off email. Shut off Facebook. Silence your phone.

Step #4: Focus on what matters.

Productivity isn't about checking off items on your to-do list. It's not about the amount of time or effort you invest in a project. Productivity is only about results and freedom. When distractions arise, remember one thing: you are supposed to be producing results and creating opportunities for more freedom in your life.

Grab a sticky note, right now, and write the following question on it: Is this activity helping me produce greater results and freedom in my business and life? Put that sticky note on your computer or desk so you'll always remember it when you get distracted.

Step #5: Let everyone know when it's work time.

Friends, family, and coworkers have good intentions, but if you don't tell them when your time needs to be respected, how can they do this? They can't. Communication is key. Once you've established your work times, tell everyone you know and ask them to help you stick to it. It's much easier when others are helping to hold you accountable as well.

Managing Information Overload

One of the biggest distractions to any entrepreneur is information overload. There is just so much content out there—new marketing, sales, and systems tactics popping up every day—it's hard not to feel like you have to learn all of them, right now.

Does that mean you shouldn't buy new courses or read industry-relevant content? No. But it does mean you should have a strategy for managing new content that comes your way. That way, you don't get distracted or bogged down with information overload.

Here are four simple ways to help you manage the information onslaught.

Create a Knowledge Acquisition Plan

Before I consume a new piece of information, I first check with my knowledge acquisition plan. This is a strategic plan that lays out the skill sets and mindset shifts I want to learn and make in my life over a specific period of time. At the start of every year, I set quarterly knowledge acquisition goals for that year. In other words, I pick four skill sets I want to master over the next twelve months in ninety-day chunks.

These skill sets could be anything related to business, relationships, health and fitness, or mindset/spirituality. Once I pick a skill set, let's say social media marketing, I research books, online programs, and other resources that will give me the information required to master this skill set.

After I've made a clearly defined knowledge acquisition plan, it's time to move onto the next step …

Create a Knowledge Implementation Plan

Have you ever bought an online course and not completed it? I have. I'm guilty as charged. The worst thing about doing this is we've just laid down hard-earned cash for a product and then not used it. There is no way we are going to benefit from it if we don't even finish the program.

Acquiring knowledge is useless if you're not implementing that knowledge to produce desired results in your life. So here's what I do ...

Once I have a new resource that I am about to consume, I set implementation goals that must be completed before moving onto the next resource. This one step forces me to take action on the information I'm learning. So if I'm reading a book about direct response marketing, I implement the strategies I learned on one of my sales pages or in my email auto responder before going onto my next resource.

This obviously takes time, so it prevents me from moving from one resource to another too quickly, limiting information overload. If you feel buried by information overload, consider creating knowledge acquisition and knowledge implementation plans. And discipline yourself to implement your newfound knowledge before moving onto the next resource.

Schedule a Time for New Blogs and Media

Occasionally, a new blog post or video will capture my attention and I will feel drawn to consume it immediately. In our age of information overload, this is unavoidable. So how do I handle it? I schedule a specific time each week—Saturday mornings—where I give myself permission to consume the new piece of content that captured my attention. Whenever I come across new content that piques my interest, I bookmark it for future reference. This keeps me focused on mastering the skill sets that are most important to me.

Implement One Thing at a Time

The fastest path to being ineffective and overwhelmed is working on too many things at the same time. For example, say you're building a new video funnel for your brand-new coaching program. Instead of trying to film the intro video, edit the header image, and write the welcome copy all at once, focus on each one of those tasks as an individual item. If you're writing copy, then just focus on all the copy you need for the site. Then edit the header image. Then handle any specific image or graphic-related work, and so on. Mixing together lots of work tasks is like pouring vodka, wine, and beer into the same glass and gulping it down. The result is going to be messy.

Action Items:

1) What times of day are you going to work? Set your schedule and stick to it for at least a week before deciding if it works for you. Reassess in a week and change it, if necessary.

2) When working, condition yourself to turn off all the distractions (phone, social media, email, etc.) so that you can focus solely on the task at hand.

3) Create a knowledge acquisition plan and knowledge implementation plan so that you minimize information overload.

4) Schedule time each week for consuming new blog posts and media that are not included in

your knowledge acquisition and implementation
plans.

Chapter 8:

Unleashing The Fearless Entrepreneur Within – How to instill "The Fearless Code" into your DNA and unleash the Fearless Mindset every single day.

You are now armed with the mindset and skill sets required to become a fearless entrepreneur. Never forget that you have the potential to create a totally badass life for yourself. You have the potential to be ultra healthy, immensely wealthy, happy and fulfilled in literally every area of your life.

However, most people will never even come close to achieving their true potential. They won't realize even a fraction of what they are capable of. Why is that? Well, this isn't a simple question and it doesn't have a simple answer. There are countless forces involved.

But one thing is certain: your ability to instill "The Fearless Code" into your DNA so that you unleash the

Fearless Mindset every single day will play a major role in the story of whether or not you unlock your immense potential and become the badass you were born to be.

The Fearless Codes

"The Fearless Codes" are the rules and laws that all fearlessly fit entrepreneurs live by. Now before I describe these codes in detail, you must understand that there are two fundamental views going on inside of you.

View number one concerns the laws you believe about yourself— that is, your perception of who you are. This self-perception is how you present yourself and act toward others.

If you believe yourself to be an infinitely powerful entrepreneur who's worth millions of dollars every single year for the value you create in the marketplace, guess how you behave? Like an entrepreneur who's worth millions of dollars because of the value you create in the marketplace.

If you believe that you are a person who is worthy to be in a relationship with a god or goddess—a person who is your equal, not your servant, not someone who is better than you, but a partner in creation—guess what happens? You start behaving in your relationship like someone who has a god or goddess as a partner and who is co-creating a powerful partnership.

If you believe that you are a powerful role model and inspiration to your children, a gateway for the way they live and lead their lives, guess what? This is exactly how you will operate when it comes to parenting.

If you believe that you are in control of your physical destiny, then you will exercise self-discipline and self-control by taking charge of what you put into your body as well as how you use your body.

Your general daily lifestyle and the small choices you make each day will be the determining factors in how well you live. No one else can do this for you. Your health relies solely on you doing what needs to be done.

You will recognize that the only real limits your body knows are the ones you give it. Your physical capabilities stretch as far as you will allow them. You will view your body as a machine that will drive itself into the vision you have for your health and fitness. With each exercise, you will strive to push yourself just a little bit harder and expand your physical capabilities just a little bit farther.

Now that you see the power in what you believe about yourself, let's consider the second view, which is what you believe about the world around you.

If you believe that the current economy is the reason you're not making the money you desire, then it doesn't matter how hard you work. It doesn't matter how much time you spend focused on your business; you have already lost the battle before it began.

If you believe that fitness is boring, then no matter how clear you get on a fitness routine, you will prevent yourself from staying committed to a routine that will surely produce results over time. If you believe it's impossible to maintain a long-term relationship that involves passion and connection, then you will end up manifesting a boring relationship that lacks passion and intimacy.

So, if you're highly committed to becoming a fearlessly fit entrepreneur, then you must start living by these seven fearless codes.

Fearless Code #1: My results are my responsibility.

In order to become a fearlessly fit entrepreneur, you need to take responsibility for your fitness. In fact, you must take responsibility for every area of your life. Once again, the key character trait that separates badasses from everyone else is self-responsibility. It's ownership. It's understanding and believing that you are the decision maker at the center of your own existence.

If you blame anything or anyone outside of yourself, including your friends, your genetics, your work environment, or anything else, you are not taking responsibility. And when you don't take responsibility, you are not going to take the actions necessary to get the results you want. If you are committed right now to become a fearlessly fit entrepreneur, the first law that you must embody is taking responsibility for your life and your actions.

Fearless Code #2: Hell yes or hell no! There's no maybe.

When you operate in the land of *maybe*, like "Let me think about this" or "Maybe I'm going to do that," it occupies all of your energy and all of your thoughts.

However, when you live in a paradigm of either "Hell yes!" or "Hell no!" you become a decisive action taker. If you really want to achieve your fitness goals, you can't dip your toe in the water. That's what you've been doing your entire life. And that's why you are not getting the results you want.

Imagine showing up in your relationships that way, with your partner or spouse, with your friends, with your family, with your business partners, with prospective clients. When you get invited to do something, or a new opportunity comes your way, you're decisive and you know what you want. You don't hesitate because you have a clear vision for your life and you make a decision right in the moment. There's either "Hell yes!" or "Hell no!"—nothing in between.

Fearless Code #3: I create time.

One of the most common excuses that entrepreneurs make for new activities, especially when it comes to fitness, is that they don't have the time. Here's the reality: no entrepreneur has the time to do anything outside of his or her business. So you have to make the choice, today, to create time and prioritize your fitness habits. Wake up an hour earlier so that you can exercise before being flooded by all the distractions of the day.

Delegate tasks in your business that you shouldn't be doing in order to free yourself up to focus on essential duties that call for your unique ability. Consider the experience of some of the busiest entrepreneurs on the planet who run billion dollar businesses. As I mentioned before, Richard Branson said the secret to his success has nothing to do with his business or how he views money—it is that he exercises every single day. Now you may have a family that requires your time and focus. You may devote time to multiple nonprofits that you care about. Even so, saying, "I don't have the time" is just an excuse that's going to limit you from taking the actions necessary to create the time. The third code or law that you must live by is taking ownership of your energy and your time by structuring your day in a way that creates time for your fitness.

Fearless Code #4: Consistency is key.

Most entrepreneurs lack energy, focus, and confidence because they haven't stayed committed to a consistent exercise and nutrition plan. I don't mean a plan where you exercise and eat right two or three days a week, or even five days a week.

I'm talking about a plan that challenges you to be in motion and sweat every single day. Consistency is the missing ingredient that will separate you from all the other people who are trying to get fit but fail.

I'm not suggesting that you have to spend hours and hours in the gym every day. Rather, I'm encouraging you to make the commitment to sweat every day. It may only take you ten or twenty minutes to work out on some days. But when you start your day with this commitment, you will skyrocket your power to produce at your highest potential in your business and you will get fit!

Fearless Code #5: Take massive action now!

Not tomorrow, not next week, right now. If your goal, right now, is to become fearlessly fit and get into the best shape of your life but you start down a thought process that puts it off—thinking to yourself, "I'm really busy this week, I've got a lot of meetings" or "I can't start now because I'm traveling"— then you'll never get started because the perfect time is an illusion. The only time is right now, in this moment. Whether it's for your fitness or your business or your relationships, you need to take a stand and assume an inner stance of someone who's action oriented and willing to do what needs to be done, today. Not tomorrow, not next week, but today.

Fearless Code #6: Create favorable conditions.

Creating favorable conditions is about shaping your environment and creating boundaries that set yourself up for success (We discussed this in detail in chapters 6 and 7.) I realize that there may be people in your life who aren't fit and healthy. There may be people who are saying, "Hey! Let's go out and get drunk tonight!" or "Let's go to happy hour!" In your work environment, you may be surrounded by people who are not healthy and completely neglect that area of their life. Maybe you are in a relationship with a partner who does not value fitness. Regardless of the negative or unsupportive people in your life, at the end of the day, it's your responsibility to minimize their impact on you.

There are three foundational pillars that have a massive impact on your health and fitness: accountability, association, and environment. Environment is what I'm talking about when it comes to creating favorable results. From this day forth, do your best to avoid blaming your partner, family, or anything else in your environment for influencing your health or fitness level. Once you take full responsibility for your environment, you will be able to create the results you desire.

Fearless Code #7: Success is a team sport.

Most entrepreneurs are self-starters and believe that they can do everything alone. I know this because this is exactly what I did in my own life, and it's what kept me stuck and led me to waste thousands of dollars and years of my life.

Although I bought books, invested in online programs, and attended seminars, I was still doing the work alone, without accountability and association. It wasn't until I invested $20,000 in myself by hiring a mentor and joining a mastermind group that I started accelerating my results.

Hiring a mentor and joining a mastermind is one of the best investments you can ever make. Having somebody in your corner who already has the results you desire will only accelerate your achievement of those results. And to do it within a group of like-minded people who are experiencing similar challenges and striving toward similar goals creates breakthroughs that would not be possible on your own

If this is something you're searching for, then I encourage you to go to thefearlesslifeacademy.com and apply for one of our upcoming events.

It doesn't matter where you are in business. I hired my first mentor the same week I lost my sole source of income (you heard this personal story in chapter 5, "Becoming Unstoppable"). It doesn't matter how many resources you have; what matters is how resourceful you are.

Can you achieve results on your own? Absolutely. But why not shorten the learning curve by investing in someone who has already created the results you desire?

As a fearless entrepreneur, you now have the sustainable energy, focus, and confidence required to take massive action in the direction of your goals despite your fears, doubts, and limiting beliefs.

You now know the essence of fear and what it truly means to have a fearless mindset. Remember, being fearless is not about the absence of fear; being fearless is having the courage to act in spite of your fears. You learned how to distinguish between the two types of fear by discovering that rational fears keep you alive and irrational fears keep you from living. You learned that fear and excitement are the exact same emotion— except that fear is excitement without the breath. You now know how to overcome the four most common fears that separate the strong from the weak, the wealthy from the poor, and the lovers from the lonely.

You understand why being fit gets you paid and the seven most commonly held limiting beliefs, lies, and excuses most entrepreneurs make about fitness. Just recognizing these seven limiting beliefs, lies, and excuses will free you up to get fit in less time without boring treadmills, painful diets, or costly gym dues. You have also discovered the fearless fitness journey and know how to apply this four-step framework to achieving goals in any area of your life.

One of the most valuable takeaways from this book is your new understanding of the true nature of money and wealth creation. You learned from Jon Butcher, Garrett Gunderson, and Jesse Elder how to transform a financial scarcity mindset into a financial abundant mindset while recognizing the true essence of financial freedom. Remember, wealth is not a number; wealth is a feeling.

You now know how to increase your internal comfort level with money so you can attract more money than you ever imagined. You learned the fastest way to lose anything (such as money, love, or happiness) is to live in fear of its loss. Above and beyond a new mindset, you are now armed with actionable wealth creation strategies that will immediately empower you to double, triple, or even increase your income tenfold. Always remember that wealth creation is a process, not an event.

You're fully aware that becoming an unstoppable entrepreneur is not for the weak willed, the lazy, or the faint of heart. If it were easy to have an extraordinary life, everyone would have one. But almost no one does, because it is not easy. It demands a lot of you. You're simply not going to achieve the life of your dreams if you fold in the face of every adversity.

Not only are you aware of the ten non-negotiable beliefs of an unstoppable entrepreneur, you're now armed with actionable strategies to incorporate these beliefs into your own mindset so that you become unstoppable too. As an unstoppable entrepreneur, you now know how to ask quality questions, minimize negative self-talk, convert fear into fuel, and create space in your mind through meditation.

Finally, you now know how to create a work environment that is optimal for peak performance. It's your time to demand more of yourself now that you've learned exactly how to demolish all the distractions that were once holding you back. From this moment forth, you will be operating from an excuse-free environment by maximizing your potential and accelerating your achievement.

I have the utmost confidence that if you implement the teachings of this book into your own life, you will attain a quality of life that was once only a dream. Thank you for investing your precious time into reading this book. I wish you tremendous success and true happiness, and I look forward to meeting you in person soon.

Live Your Life Fearlessly,

Peter

Special Bonus Offer

If you haven't done so already, I encourage you to take advantage of my bonus gifts that were mentioned at the beginning of this book.

Visit www.thefearlessmindsetbook.com to download your FREE BOOK BONUSES that include:

- The Unstoppable Entrepreneur quiz
- The Fearless Fitness Challenge four-part video series
- Expert interviews with some of the world's fittest entrepreneurs
- The Fearless Life goal/habit tracking sheet

EXCLUSIVE INVITATION: The Fearless Life Academy

If you're interested in radically accelerating your results, I encourage you to consider attending the three-day Fearless Life Academy. At the Fearless Life Academy, we will dive deeper into the insights provided in this book and you will discover:

- How to create a fearless mindset so that you can consistently take massive action in the direction of your dreams despite your fears, doubts, and limiting beliefs

- A step-by-step blueprint to get fit in less time than you ever thought possible without boring treadmills, painful diets, or costly gym dues
- Daily habits and rituals that skyrocket your energy, focus, and confidence so that you MAKE MORE MONEY in your business
- How to double your income by generating more leads for your business and converting them into paying clients
- How to position yourself as an authority so that you can raise your rates
- How to reconnect with your masculine edge resulting in more connected sex in your love relationship
- Communication strategies to reignite the passion, romance, and desire in your love relationship while minimizing conflict

By the end of the course, you will possess the certainty and confidence to handle anything life throws at you. You will feel more self-assured and powerful, and you will be prepared to take more decisive action than ever before.

Whether you are currently a millionaire, middle-class, or broke, if you're not 100% satisfied with your income, your body, your relationship, your level of happiness, and you know you have more potential than your results are showing, then register for the Fearless Life Academy today at
www.thefearlesslifeacademy.com.

About the Author

Peter Scott IV is the founder of the Fearless Life Academy and creator of the 90-Day Fearless Fitness Challenge. He is one of the world's top mindset and fitness mentors for high-achieving entrepreneurs.

Peter's life was consumed by fear at a very young age, having to tell his mother at ten years old that she was no longer suitable to raise him because of her alcoholism. And later, having to watch his father give up on life and drink himself to death.

Since then, he has dedicated his life to empowering others to leverage fitness as a tool to overcome their fears, doubts, and limiting beliefs.

Peter now mentors high-achieving entrepreneurs to get fit in less time so that they can double their income and become unstoppable.